I0879239

Confluences 2

Essays on the New Canadian Literature

edited by
Nurjehan Aziz

MAWENZI
HOUSE

©2017 The Authors

Except for purposes of review, no part of this book may be reproduced in any form without prior permission of the publisher.

We acknowledge the support of the Canada Council for the Arts for our publishing program. We also acknowledge support from the Government of Ontario through the Ontario Arts Council.

ONTARIO ARTS COUNCIL
CONSEIL DES ARTS DE L'ONTARIO
an Ontario government agency
un organisme du gouvernement de l'Ontario

Canada Council for the Arts
Conseil des arts du Canada

Cover design by Angel Guerra/Archetype

Library and Archives Canada Cataloguing in Publication

Confluences 2 : essays on the new Canadian literature / edited by Nurjehan Aziz.

Includes bibliographical references.
Issued in print and electronic formats.
ISBN 978-1-988449-18-0 (softcover).--ISBN 978-1-988449-19-7 (HTML)

1. Canadian literature--20th century--History and criticism. 2. Canadian literature--21st century--History and criticism. 3. Essays. I. Aziz, Nurjehan, editor II. Title: Confluences two. III. Title: Essays on the new Canadian literature.

PS8117.C665 2017 C810.9'0054 C2017-905393-0
C2017-905394-9

Printed and bound in Canada by Coach House Printing.

Mawenzi House Publishers Ltd.
39 Woburn Avenue (B)
Toronto, Ontario M5M 1K5
Canada
www.mawenzihouse.com

Contents

Preface

This second volume of the Confluences series continues the exposition, by established as well as a new generation of literary critics, of some of the most exciting new writing to emerge in Canada in the last four decades, following the postcolonial wave of immigration of the 1960s and 70s. The "new writing" defined by this series draws its inspiration, in some form, from the histories, cultures, traditions, and experiences of the countries of Asia, Africa, the Middle and Near East, and the Caribbean—i.e. areas considered historically outside the purview of the "Western." Much has changed recently, of course, but much remains the same. Employing a variety of approaches and bringing together multiple concerns—memory, history, and concentric identities; the subordination of women and strategies of liberation in South Asia; the legacies of racism and Japanese internment in Canada; Chinatown as geography, repository, and inspiration—this new body of writing collectively continues to redefine the idea of Canadian Literature, prompting this nation to continue, unabashedly, to look at itself anew. The essays in this and the previous volume are meant to prompt further serious discussion of this writing and to bring greater exposure to its authors. We expect to continue with more such expositions in Confluences 3 and 4, in our belief that only by critical appraisal and reflection does a literature establish itself.

DIONNE BRAND

"This dock is my dock": Dionne Brand's Room of Light

Franca Bernabei

In the course of several interviews during her life-long dedication to writing (poetry, short stories, novels, one novella, and nonfiction), Dionne Brand has progressively offered her readers an approach to the reasoning and motivations that underlie her creative imagination. This self-reflexive critical activity girds the composite text of *A Map to the Door of No Return* (2001), whose flexible form, loosely inspired by the cartographic model announced in the title, crisscrosses narration and meditation, essay and poetry, life and travel-writing and historical, archaeological, and geographical probing. It comes as no surprise, therefore, that Brand's most recent work, an equally composite but formally more unified text, should now interrogate more extensively the import of her literary production. Her readership cannot but treasure the further insight that *The Blue Clerk* (2018) offers for a better understanding of her creative trajectory. However, what is striking and definitely intriguing about it, is the *savoir* by means of which Brand succeeds in modulating a poetics that is not only inspired by pre-existing texts but is rather produced in and through the process of writing itself, intertwining multiple levels of meaning and referential fields, and translating into poetic prose the author's political, affective, and aesthetic involvement in the human condition of Blacks and all those who have been oppressed, classified, or excluded, by the hegemonic and racist programme of modernity. Any attempt to disentangle the connectivity of these various levels (poetics, aesthetics at large, linguistics, rhetoric, politics, and political philosophy, historical reappraisals of European structures of domination and their conceptual foundations, botanical and natural science, life- and travel-writing) may in the end prove frustrating and even deleterious for an appreciation of the whole. And yet Brand's reader cannot but accept the challenge to pursue, through a singular act of reading that works "from" and "with" these entangled levels, the clues that are adroitly disseminated throughout the text, both by means of explicit statements and by more covert allusions.

A Small Blue Book

The Blue Clerk straightforwardly presents itself as an *ars poetica.* But notice the small letters. While it is indeed an *ars poetica*, Brand's "*ars*"—as we might well have suspected—is much more than a poetic treatise. It is ultimately composed by the "alternate spelling" (Verso 47) of her writing and the specificity of her Black, diasporic, critical standpoint. As a matter of fact, as it hints more than once, it is "the small blue book of the author's thoughts" ("Stipule"). In addition, several factors contribute to this peculiar appropriation of Horace's canonical treatise, conceived as a poetic epistle addressed to friends who lacked literary expertise.

To start with, according to the title, and the evoked discursive genre, Brand's "treatise" should consist of a collection of verses. Actually, it is composed of meticulously numbered and "unnumbered" prose units of different length and purport that retain the association with poetry suggested in the paratext. However, these units are defined as "versos," that is, the left-hand pages that pile up in the course of the gestation and production of a literary work. The adoption of this both referential and metaphorical field allows the author to bring to the fore the amount of labour (collecting, selecting, including, and excluding) that, like a ship's cargo, weighs the act of writing down. As we will see, the evocation of cargo is not casual. Indeed, it helps to contextualize the scene of writing itself. But for the moment let's consider this passage from the unnumbered verso, titled "Stipule," that introduces *The Blue Clerk*:

> I have withheld more than I have written. I have restrained more than I have given. I have left unsaid more than I have

> said. I have withheld much more than I have withheld . . . I will have parsed the structure of the sentence and the meaning of the sentence and reformulated it to resolve some understanding that was tentative in the first place, but that merely for the sake of agreeing to a rule of syntax I present as certain. Moreover, I will have cleaned out all of my doubt, or all of my prevarication, or all of my timidity. Or all of me.

No doubt this statement, both a personal confession and a warning to (and perhaps a stipulation to) the reader, paradoxically both anticipates and undermines the construct that lies ahead. On the one hand, it evinces the impossible task of adequately translating into words the perceptual, sensory quality of "the author's thoughts" described further on as "cubic metres of senses, perceptions and, resistant facts . . . some of these are quite dangerous and some of them are too delicate and beautiful for the present world" (Verso 1).

On the other hand, the passage showcases the hesitations, uncertainties and conflicting emotions that feed the magmatic ground of (Black) subjectivity and only find a syntactical, functional and constrictive resolution once they are arranged as words and sentences on the written page. Thus, through the process of writing, this discursive self signifies that its selfhood is both constructed and dispersed in language: it can "come into its own only in, and as, another, an alterity" (Richter 221). In the last analysis, Brand's *ars poetica* is based on the tension between this double movement of construction and dispersal as well as on a latency, or silence; since "[w]riting is a negotiation between what is said and what is unsaid, between what is written and what is withheld" ("Stipule"), a negotiation embodied in the dialogical interplay between "the author" (sometimes further specified as "the poet") and "the blue clerk" of the title.

In this way, Brand's "treatise," far from offering a didactic—albeit magnanimous—collection of prescriptions to the "unversed" reader, is the product of the relation (even mis-relation) that intradiegetically connects double pronominal subjects (the "she" and the "I" of author and clerk) to the "you" of their respective interlocutors. Albeit only occasionally, subject and object, "I" and "you," admittedly coincide: "Now you are sounding like me, the clerk says. I am you, the author says" (Verso 1.1.01).

Or, more provocatively, the "small blue book of the author's thoughts" itself becomes the elusive threshold of this pronominal conflation. In fact, "The blue clerk lost the small book of her thoughts. It was the one book she wrote herself" (Verso 37) is followed by "When I lost the blue book of your blue thoughts . . . " (Verso 37.1)

As a whole, the constant, and sometimes even disconcerting, slippage from one level of enunciation and its relative structure of address to the other establishes and embodies an intersecting and dialogical, or antiphonal, hermeneutics—a (self)-reflexive interpreting activity that suggests above all the elusiveness, or fragility, of the "I" that "stipulates" the pact with the reader. This elusiveness then resurfaces in statements such as "I am unpinned from all allegiances. Of course I'm not. But what if I wrote like this?" (Verso 5.5); or, "I put my whole life's work . . . into attending to the new assignments for entry. The 'I' that I am talking about is not me, of course . . . " (Verso 16.5) The divarication between the "I" that writes "I" and the textual and historical "I" points, on the one hand, to the pressures of history and society on the integrity of a (the) Black, diasporic, even "barbar[ic]" (Verso 32.1) woman self and her "controversial"[1] attempt at "mak[ing] a way through life" (Verso 3.3). On the other hand, this divarication exposes the responsibility that the *poiétés* (maker), as a depository of the brutality of the past, a witness of its legacy in the contemporary "scene of the real" (Verso 16.3), and a visitor of the sites of terror disseminated throughout the world, assumes with respect to the choice and deployment of her subject matter.

Indeed, occasionally conflicting observations concerning the efficacy of poetry—or better, the possibility of making poetry in today's "ravaged world" (as Brand labels it in *Inventory*), and poetically resuscitating the subjects that aspire to new paths of liberation, recognition, and citizenship—constellate the versos. Certainly, in comparison to prose, the versos express a belief in the generative, restorative, and revealing power of poetic language and its wider possibilities of negotiating "between what is said, what is written and what is withheld" (Verso 19). Various etymological clues disseminated in the headings of the versos highlight not only the generative force connected with the verb *poiein* and its derivatives but also the activity inherent to the semantic field of terms such as *verse* (as I mentioned above) and *strophe*. Other times, however, the dialogue between author and clerk evinces a sort of disillusionment, or skepticism, about the agency of this medium, especially when a meditative, and (self-)reflexive mood prevails over the argumentative and the speculative. And not only poetry as medium ("I depend on something so thin, says the author, so thin" [Verso 34.1]) but also language itself is questioned as a consequence of the disciplinary regime that still "occupies"[2] Black experience and subjects and "abjects" the Black body:

> I am trying to find a language, yes, the author says, a language without . . . I am trying to find a thought, the clerk says, a thought without . . . a thought unburdened of all you are burdened with. (Verso 16.7)

> I no longer know what language I speak or whether this one is the original. I no longer exist, it seems, anywhere. (Verso 16.8)

In these instances (and not only, because this mood reverberates on the whole) the real addressee of Brand's *ars poetica* seems to be not so much the reader as "me": "all this overtakes *me*" (Verso 33.1); "I have a photo of *me* who is *me*, and then there is the *me* who is *me*" (Verso 40.2); "I am not really in life, the author says. I am really a voyeur. But the part of *me* that is in life is in pain all the time. That's *me* says the clerk. You watch, I feel" (Verso 42, emphasis mine). "Me," then, signifies that most intimate, elusive, and sentient core of the writing self, the self that withholds, the self that mediates, rather than synthesizes, between life and work, author and clerk, and historical and textual subject. In the last analysis, the exchange of the author-clerk's now complementary now divergent now coincident and now self-mirroring ruminations modulates what we may define as the author's philosophy of perception as well as her aesthetic creed. Her thought rubs against the foundations of Western epistemology in such a way that story and discourse, language, meaning and experience, and phenomenological and historical consciousness are constantly confronted, interrogated, and put to the test. Nevertheless, Brand's writing, as I hope to demonstrate, is much more than a "writing back."

"How do I get out of this zoo?"

While the author acknowledges a debt to Kamau Brathwaite's poetics, which she describes as the "Condensed smoke of a luminous flame. Black equilibrium Black spun" (Verso 13.1), she also appreciates the work of writers of the Americas such as Jacques Roumain, Gabriel Garcia Marquez, and Ralph Ellison, the scope and freshness of which extends beyond time and place.[3] In her view, these writers represent the only credible response to the "toxic" imagination, the dehumanizing and regulatory cultural practices of the present. In particular, the author acknowledges her closeness to Ralph Ellison, "the only one who has written a book entirely of left-hand pages," a book the absurdism of which reflects the repressive machine that has evacuated the protagonist's body and will and still controls its interpretation (Verso 21.4). Also the creationist creed of the Chilean poet Vicente Huidobro who, in his "Arte Poètica" warned that we must "watch" the "word" in order to invent new "worlds," is evoked in Verso 46, while other versos acknowledge the vitality of the paintings of the African Americans Jacob Lawrence ("a call to the future," Verso 17) and Romare Bearden, the Haitian American Basquiat (Verso 3.1), the Spanish Mexican Remedio Varo (Verso 16.3) and the Cuban Wifredo Lam (Verso 17.2). Ultimately, it is the art of the beloved jazz composers John Coltrane, Thelonius Monk, and Charles Mingus—whose political and philosophical charge still needs, in the author-clerk's view, to be "translated"—that is repeatedly evoked and advocated for its liberatory, "detoxifying" power (Verso 17). The more so that the post-September 11 North American scene appears even more culturally policed, "dormant, archival, fiduciary" (Verso 21.1). Actually, jazz serves as a model for composing poetry itself: a whole verso (Verso 14) consists in a *lectio magistralis* that dissects the musical/rhetorical strategies of Coltrane's "Venus" and explains their impact on the metrical and discursive structure of *Ossuaries.*[4]

While Brand's *The Blue Clerk* is conceptually grounded on the composite, transamerican aesthetics outlined above, her own *ars* educes a distressed, perhaps even distrustful, and certainly watchful poetics of emergency, where the invention (the emergence) of the word ("A word is not an easy thing" Verso 44) is always already engaged in a confrontation with the "humanist narrative" (Verso 16.3) and the imperialist, homogenizing aesthetics of modernity. The "secret architecture" of the latter and "poetry, itself" (16.1)—as expressed in major modernist figures such as Charles Baudelaire (and his commentators), Apollinaire, T S Eliot, and Gertrude Stein—are revisited and contested for their appropriation of and humiliating approach to African art and Black people, alongside the omissions identified in Walter Benjamin's discussion of commodification in his renowned Arcades project.

Indeed, crucial to the indictment of the underlying assumptions that predicated the ontology and biopolitics of modernity is the author's focus on the historical moment in which "human zoos" were established in order to observe, measure, categorize, and exhibit "exotic" Black bodies. In *A Map to the Door of No Return* Brand discusses the cognitive scheme through which Blacks perceive their corporeality in terms of captivity—a captivity historically marked by the passage through that material and "mythic" door of the slave trade and perpetuated culturally and socially in the present (35-41). The versos devoted to the genesis and poetics of *Ossuaries* attribute a retrospective foundational significance to the rise of human zoos that reduced people to objects of observation and consumption: "There in the zoos, humanity is defined in the modern. Who is without, and who is within . . . And how do they perform the body? They performed the animal; fossilized in spirit" (Verso 16.1). According to Michel-Rolph Trouillot, the creation of "facts" is the first step in the Western construction of history (26). In Brand's call for "reshap[ing] all kinds of understandings" (Verso 15.1) this "fact," which Benjamin seemingly overlooked, has been essential for the formation (and de-formation) of both author and clerk: "That is when I left you, the clerk says, that is when I created you, the author says, that is when I created you, the clerk says, that is when you left me the author says" (Verso 16.3). The chiasmic spiral of rebounding and rebutting assertions marks a divide between a before and an after in the poet's consciousness: "the death of the aesthetic of imperialism . . . that contains narratives of the body, bodies that the poet suggests were dead anyway" (ibid); the death of "the former poet" (ibid) and the inception of a "double seeing" (ibid), a sort of phenomenological perception of oneself as still being on display in the world;[5] a body "deconstructed as itself, and reconstructed as a set of practices in un-freedom" (ibid).

Using a womanist, and more specifically historical and aesthetic, perspective to develop Fanon's denunciation of the crumbling of the "negro" corporeal schema and its replacement by a "racial epidermal schema" (112) under the gaze of the white man, the poet admits that she can only provide a glimpse of these "bits and pieces" (Verso 16.3) that actually are "corpses of the humanist narrative" (ibid)—"bags of muscle and fat and bones that are utilized . . . to demonstrate the ethical development of a certain subject whom is not we" (ibid). And yet, in spite of the clerk's objections, and the Foucauldian skein of regulation, surveillance, and detention enacted in a subsequent verso—("I went . . . to all the commissions. I said, here is my body . . . my shattered self. Shatterings. I call them; my limbs, my ankles, my jaw . . . I insist on my innocence" Verso 16.8)—her responsibility—"I am aware, always aware, clinically aware" [Verso 16.6]—is to refuse "to live in that world anymore" (Verso 16.3). In fact, she must keep seeing,[6] seeing the chasm that fissures the "so-called reality and the scene of the real" (ibid). If Merleau-Ponty posits the primacy of our perceptual experience as "the primordial operation which impregnates sensible being with a meaning" (McCleary xii), the meaning that the author extracts from this operation is tainted by the freight of what she sees, and what it means to see, because "[t]oday everything has the sediment of experience, the cumulus of event tinges the new experience, or summarises it before it is felt, or alters it before it is observed" (Verso 39).

In his essay "On Some Motifs in Baudelaire," Walter Benjamin laments the atrophy of *Erfahrung*, the sedimentation of often unconscious contents in memory that connects the individual and the collective past. He attributes this atrophy to the advent of industrial capitalism and the pervasiveness of commodities.[7] The author, on the other hand, debates with the clerk the destruction of a form of experience that was already dead and the *long durée* of a past that is not yet past: "so much debris . . . It repeats without resolution. No one wants to hear about it anymore, but it stays in the air. I wake up and it's there, I go to sleep and it is there, I look out on the garden and it is there. It's invisible like the debris around our planet now but it's there, emitting shafts of pink and green light through the atmosphere . . . I wish this would be over so I can get on with my life. How long do these centuries last" (Verso 22).[8] She grieves over the atrophy of *Erlebnis*—the lived, punctual experience of her young, tender self, "unassailable, undiminished, unsedimented, raw and conscious" (Verso 39).[9]

Ars botanica

By exploiting the multiple meanings of the noun "verso," which seems to allude in Brand's own spelling (see the Index) to the back of a leaf, the manuscript may superimpose *ars poetica* and *ars botanica* in a way that reminds us of Goethe's science of morphology, the aim of which was to establish a homology between aesthetic appraisal and the epistemology of science. However, as we will see, no archetypal research of this homology is pursued in *The Blue Clerk*, although both the botanical world and the world of the natural sciences insinuate themselves not only in the headings but also throughout the versos. The recourse to a binomial nomenclature for plants and animals showcases the impact Linnaeus's "taxonomic gaze" (Müller-Wille 37) had on the reconfiguration of nature in the course of the eighteenth and nineteenth centuries. More than that, it reminds us of how science and empire went hand in hand (Lafuente and Valverde 134); how the concept of species in the animal and vegetable kingdoms, their differentiation by morphology (137), and the subsumption of the varieties of nature as specimens under larger taxa (139) brought about a unification of knowledge that minimized distances between near and far (137) and purged it of all context-dependent meaning (Müller-Wille 46). Nomenclature displaced traditional wisdom and native names, and botanical policy became political botany (Lafuente and Valverde 138, 142).

In this light, the wharf becomes the stage on which the process of writing—that marks the transition from experience to the experience of *ècriture*—is enacted by the dialogical interplay between author and clerk, thereby acquiring an even more allusive resonance. The symbolic import of this setting is patently admitted, in the same way as Ralph Ellison's room of light in *The Invisible Man* is his: "this dock is my dock," says the author (Verso 21.4). Ellison's clerk "lived underground and selected many pages sent above"—but in the end "retained all those documents" that were discovered after his death "and assembled erroneously" (ibid). Alternately, Brand's "ink-drenched" (Verso 1, 4) clerk keeps pacing up and down the dock, expecting the arrival of a ship, preparing for one, inspecting the bales of paper that have been piling up for years, shifting "old left-handed pages to the back, making room for the swift, voluminous, incoming freight" (ibid). Not unlike Ellison's invisible man secluded in his warm hole underground, in a border area between Harlem and the city, the clerk, except "for the insects and the dormant and dead plants," is the only inhabitant of the dock (Verso 12), located "somewhere, at a port, somewhere" (Verso 1). Actually, "[t] he clerk understands that this wooden dock is attached to nothing; no land, no town, no city. She notices the bryozoan colonies growing on the joists. Their starburst cilia waving, their gelatinous rooms expanding" (Verso 21.2). Besides, "[t]here are green unclassified aphids" (Verso 1) living with the papers, aphids that later on appear in the author's "real garden" (Verso 51) and whose writing she will be able to decipher.

This half-dead, half-alive scenario, drenched in ink and yet pullulating with the gelatinous and unyielding presence of both classified and unclassified animal species, looms as a haunting, imaginative foil for the myriad wharfs and docks that provided the historical stage for the departures and arrivals of the slave ships. It also evokes the activity of those ships that "collect[ed] boxes, books, gardens, and greenhouses . . . mobilized to collect, record, and move nature from place to place" (Schiebinger and Swan 13) under the aegis of the "scientifico-colonial machine" (5). Nonetheless, Brand has no intention to embrace the system of global botanical exchange that reduced plants to specimens, numbers and names and made them interchangeable (Müller-Wille 38). On the contrary, her *ars botanica* suggests that human beings cannot be separated from the living matter they share with other forms of life on earth. As the polymath Thomas Sebeok has taught us, the world of signs embraces plant life (phytosemiosis), animal life (zoosemiosis), and human life (anthroposemiosis) in a single life-world continuum (biosemiosis).

John Deely, another student of semiotic processes, suggests that we broaden literary semiotics to include natural phenomena as well. Indeed, Brand's articulation of "form," and the commonalities that "traverse" (one of the possible meanings of the verb *verse*, Verso 4) supposedly distinct realms, seems to favor this continuum rather than Goethe's archetypal research on morphology. The action of her word (in Huidobro's sense) interlaces a number of conventionally distinct worlds: the plant and the animal, the literary and the linguistic; and the biological and the evolutionary. In effect, her writing weaves these worlds into an all-embracing semiosphere that, albeit more intuitive and imaginative than descriptive, alters the significance of their respective disciplinary ranks. Thus, the almost uncanny semanticization of the wharf makes of it both an alternative scene of inquiry with respect to the contexts and settings in which the sciences operate (Bhambra 16) and the ground on which the semantic, in the form of discourse, emerges from "the pure pre-babble language," or "semiotic sea" of nature (Agamben 64).

Experimentum linguae

As I argued at the outset, the "stipule" that opens the text (botanically defined in the heading as "a small leaf like appendage to a leaf" ("Stipule") lends itself to a nonbotanical implication. However, botanical nuances surface when the "freight of withholding" is referred to as being "[e]vergreen and deciduous" (ibid), while its literal meaning—of an appendage that may or may not be part of a plant and associated with the "unnumbering" of the verso in question—apparently downsizes but actually magnifies the import of this introductory statement. The more so that "stipule" reappears a few pages later as the heading of another verso that consists of a short, dazzling string of predominantly nominal phrases that flashes forth a (self-)portrait of the author "washed in emergency," fragments of her past, inventories drawn from the animal and plant world and lists of things needed by author and clerk. In addition, we are given thematic clues ("unclassified ways of saying . . . are we not human . . . unnumbered," "Stipule") that will serve as sources for subsequent meditations.

This, in a nutshell, is what the small blue book of the author's thoughts is about. And the reader is solicited to "decipher" the "gradatios of violet, blue and black" (ibid) of its language as well as the movement of its stunning juxtapositions and associations, reiterations and allusive echoes, all of which signal the need to elaborate new conceptual metaphors capable of subverting the hierarchical taxonomies (and biopolitics) of colonial botany as well as the classifications and categorizations of the human still at work today. This taxonomic subversion of meaning that glimmers in and between words seems to posit a single life-world continuum, where each form of life delineates its own environment according to its unique web of relations (von Uexküll 55) and gestures towards a reconfiguration of the cognitive patterns and forms of understanding that have brought about the "unfinished project" of modernity.

Thus language becomes both experience and experiment, recognition of the visible and apprehension, or comprehension, of the invisible ("a substrata of life that people are unaware of" [Verso 6.1]); a tool for critique and a site of inquiry—indeed, language understood as a diacritical means of reading and writing differentially (Kearney 3).[10] Brand also interrogates language in its various articulations: as the voice of a baby, a pure sound from within provided with its own intelligence, "before alphabets" and grammar (Verso 27); or as the internal voice from without, condensed in a "hmm," a sound that is already a sentence with its admonishing, cautionary warning (Verso 25.1); or as the power of a single word, the word "but" (Verso 44)—the understanding of which is retrospectively acknowledged to have marked a before and after in the perception of the author's younger self (Verso 4). Language also incarnates the interface of a "suprasubjective" (Deely 118) "biosemiosis" that intersects the animal and human sphere: "The clerk is noiseless, silent, soundless, intent on the marsupial sighs of each letter of the alphabet. Ah, she says. Within the letter 'a' for example, a perfect pouch for adipose, for aleph, for amen, for ah, for water" (Verso 54). And language includes the effort of speech, as the Index suggests, forced to establish those phonemic oppositions that progressively will lead towards the discrimination of signs and the discriminating knowledge transmitted through words:

> Do you know the butchery it requires to skin the vocal tract for the soft, perfumed sliver of an h? The velar k, the bilabial p? Then, to circumlocute the corona of the tongue for T and Th and S? That is the clerk's job, and then, with the same professional alacrity of a slaughterer, to apprehend the constituting

> words and sift these for the unchastened perceptions, the incurable knowledges of who we are. (Verso 11)

The clerk asks the author, "Why do you talk like that? Where did you get that voice?" And the author replies, "I collected it . . . From everything" (Verso 47). What the phrase "from everything" means is expressed through an incantatory, paratactic chain of nouns, verbs, and prepositions that disarticulates ready-made significations and re-articulates them according to a different "music." "Everything" is the Caribbean, the site where the "I" that writes "I" locates the origin of her discourse. What it meant to be born and "talk" in that context to a child shines through the "lateral relation of one sign to another which makes each of them significant so that meaning appears only at the intersection of and as it were in the interval between words" (Merleau-Ponty 42). In this way Merleau-Ponty explains the correlation between language and silence, between what is said and what is not said. In Brand's text, meaning appears first and foremost by means of an intentional act that sets up a nexus between an expression and an experiential content, and it is Caribbean experience that gives expression its meaning (Violi 71).[11] Thus, the intersecting, interacting semiosis mentioned above has its defining generative power:

> Why do you speak that way? Because of water, the reef out there, the frigate magnificens, look at the boiling turquoise, the sea's albumen. Because the throat fills with thick reeds, drowned fine pebbles, because of stairs's gradient, the way corn is disappearing, steep terraces. Grapheme teeth, on the cold walls and the stringy aortas, a thousand musics. (Verso 47)

Nevertheless, the effort of speech, or, rather, the effort to stir up "the racist alphabets of narratives—the prevalent modes of speech and key impediments to black being"[12] haunts the author's and clerk's sleep:

> The author and clerk spoke in their sleep. At times nouns were haunted by prepositions followed by an adjective . . . Alphabets were used up and used up and lay flat and slumped, and dishevelled of their normal shapes. It's useless to speak any other way, the author says in a morning voice. Useless says the clerk. The night passed in more nouns. (Verso 47)

What the author is "speaking" about is the "alternate spelling of everything" (ibid) embodied by the "lists" that admittedly she cherishes and of which the verso in question offers an example. Contrary to this verso, the lists that are scattered throughout the text are mostly extracted from the clerk's "almanac of colours" (Verso 10.3), and they inflect and celebrate the infinite forces of attraction that make up a blue, violet, and lemon language. It is this language of colours that revises the classical precept *ut pictura poesis* and may remind us, instead, of Goethe's imaginative, physico-sensorial theory of colours.

"Every listing generates a new listing. Every map another road"

Once again, the dock is the ground or interface that sets in motion a web of meanings connecting the endosomatic (nature) and the esosomatic (culture) (Agamben 64), the words of colours and the colours of words:

> The dock is. The clerk thinks. Lemon summary, lemon factors. In the lemon distance are lemon wasps in lemon objections. Antipodal green, brindle marrow, marrow's satellite. What are you saying, the author says. Lemon hydrogen, the clerk thinks insecticides. Lemon files. (Verso 17.2)

Indeed, this soundless, ostensive language "de-monstrates" how the colours that compose the almanac are "different modalities of our co-existence with the world" (Merleau-Ponty 5) and at the same time respond, as it were, to their own cognitive and affective surroundings. Not for nothing are the "blue" clerk and the small "blue" book given such an opaque and yet transparent relevance. But it is Verso 55[13] in which author and clerk reflect on the former's "pilgrimage" to the Door of No Return, that most intriguingly addresses "an unformulated power of deciphering within us."[14] "When I finally arrived at the door of no return, there was an official there . . . he was authoritative. Exhausted violet, the clerk interjects. Yes, he was, says the author. Violet snares . . . Violet files. Violet chemistry. Violet unction." As to the gods—the ghosts or absent presences ("They lay in their corners, on their disintegrated floors, they lay on their walls of skin dust") of those who were kept segregated in the castle before being stacked in the ships—"They looked at us like violet;

like violet teas they drank us. We said, here we are. They said, you are still alive. We said, yes, yes we are still alive. How lemon, they said, how blue like fortune" (Verso 55). This language of colour communicates the impact of an experience of the sacred that cannot (should not) be said, cannot (should not) be spoken. While it reaches here its emotional climax, it also folds back upon itself, demanding that we look for its meaning laterally and obliquely, in the cycles of repetition, (re)elaboration and restating[15] embodied in the ecstatic, anti-hierarchical, rhyzomatic strings that constitute many of the versos.[16]

If the dock "is," then lists "exist" (Verso 47). Their numberless, unexpected combinations of adjective and noun counter the lists, arranged alphabetically and numbered serially, of the scientists' collections of data and "cycles of accumulation" (Müller-Wille 45, 46), and disrupt the conventional relations of alphabet to grammar, names to exemplar, and signifiers to signifieds. In other words, the poetics enacted by *The Blue Clerk* is not just a pictorial rendition of the scene of the real;[17] rather it shakes the expressive potentialities of language in order to tear a new sound from it.[18] "Harmolodics," according to free-jazz musician Ornette Coleman, means that "harmony, melody, speed, rhythm, time and phrases all have equal position in the results that come from the placing and spacing of ideas."[19] And it is precisely by spacing, placing (and displacing) her ideas in the "consecutive or serial or alternative" (Verso 47) rhythm of the lists that the author brings forth an acoustic, translucent, and "harmolodic" truth (a call for the human, a call for freedom, a call for Black citizenship) that is both liberatory and upsetting. Therefore, if Brand's *ars poetica* demands to be read against the grain of a centuries-long tradition of denial of Black humanity, it also demands to be "seen" and listened to in the uniqueness of its polysemic, diacritical hermeneutics.

In the last analysis, it is the very fragmentary structure of this "small blue book" that formally and conceptually holds it together, in the sense that the autonomy of the single versos bespeaks their relationship to the whole. More specifically, the presence of lists, which, as we have seen, seem to test and thrive on the infinitude of language, showcases their accretive connection to the larger unit in which they are embedded rather than interrupt sequence. In addition, the very shapelessness of the list suggests that there is always more to it. While it ends, it does not conclude. Even the final list, that list of listings (Belknap 2) that is the Index—aptly denominated "Index 1"—is provisional (improvisational) and, so to speak, in progress, writing and re-writing itself. In fact, instead of concluding, it is followed by a verso, in first person, that bears the same number (Verso 33.1) of a previous one and re-presents its content in a more concise form. What that verso is about is a primary scene of grace, scarcity and longing—the occurrence of which, we may presume, is accretive and inconclusive, embedded as it is in the author-clerk's archival memory. It is in repeated scenes like this that a whole universe of meaning is contained in a shard of memory ("a patch of corn," "a small zinnia bed," "a wrecked mattress," Verso 33.1). Such shards figure and re-figure what the author "knew, and felt, and sensed" as a child.[20] As she explains, "My job is to be completely uncomfortable, as painful and as horrible and sometimes as personally devastating as all that might be. You always have to distrust the comfort of solutions" (Verso 15.1). Nevertheless, her "uncomfortable" poetics vividly resonates both with the impact of its "crude thinking"[21] and the beauty of the "blue," "worried" notes—sung or played in a slightly off-pitch Jazz—of its *écriture.*

I would like to thank Dionne Brand for allowing me to read the manuscript of The Blue Clerk *before publication. The book will be published in 2018 by McClelland and Stewart and Duke University Press.*

WAYSON CHOY

Between (Hi)Story and Space: Wayson Choy's Postmodern Chinatown

Jason Wang

Wayson Choy's *Paper Shadows: A Chinatown Memoir* (1999) is a literary journey revisiting the author's past through memory while also reconstructing it. Intimate, nostalgic, and playfully ironic, Choy's self-portrait aims to unravel the importance of Chinatown in his understanding of himself as a Chinese Canadian writer. The work begins with a real-life mystery and a quest for identity prompted by a mysterious phone call to the middle-aged author:

> "I saw your mother last week."
>
> The stranger's voice on the phone surprised me. She spoke firmly, clearly, with the accents of Vancouver's Old Chinatown: "I saw your *mah-ma* on the street."
>
> Not possible. This was 1995. Eighteen years earlier I had sat at a St Paul's Hospital bed beside Mother's skeletal framework while she lay gasping for breath: the result of decades of smoking. . . .
>
> "You must be mistaken," I said, confident that this woman would recognize her error and sign off.
>
> "No, no, not your mother"—the voice persisted—"I mean your *real* mother." (3-4)

With the realization that he may have been adopted, and that the loving parents he believed to be his biological family had perhaps shrouded his identity in secrecy, the narrator begins to look towards Chinatown to recuperate his past. As he navigates through the Chinatown of his boyhood, he unfolds layers of stories and some mysteries; he recalls the bodily experience of long-vanished places, such as theatres and stores. The title of the book is playful yet ambiguous: paper is a Chinese invention but it assumes multiple meanings in this memoir. He recalls the paper snake toy that gave him pleasure in Ming Wo's Hardware store and the falsified paper documents that were often required to circumnavigate racist, exclusionary immigration laws. The title alerts us to the "paper brides," women who appropriated the legal papers of the deceased to immigrate to Canada. In *Paper Shadows*, the identities proclaimed on official paperwork are not always genuine.

Through the gaze of the narrator's memory, the reader can picture a Chinese immigrant family in 1940s Vancouver living within a few blocks of Chinatown, the father often away working as a cook on a Canadian Pacific steamship liner, the mother staying home to take care of the five-year-old son. Choy writes:

> Mother adjusted unwillingly to Father's long absences at sea. Each time he returned, she would wait up for him, however late his arrival. When thick fog or storms delayed him, she still waited up. (37)

This waiting scene is typical in the everyday life of the Chinese diasporic community in Canada, reflecting the author's own story of his childhood—a retrospective construction of himself in a complex narrative in which the spatial metaphors of Chinatown merge with his personal family stories. These stories are the imaginative building blocks of this postmodern *Bildungsroman* and *Künstlerroman*: the story of the writer's development as a Chinese Canadian, a fable of identity, a postmodern threading of the real and the imagined, the fragmented and the open-ended. Like many stories of historiographic metafiction, this memoir relies on a mixture of identity and imagination, mythology and reality, nostalgia and irony.

Wayson Choy was born Choy Way Sun on April 20, 1939, in Vancouver, as he announces in his introduction, giving us "the documented facts," which are based, as he writes in the same paragraph, on "the *false paper names*, officially recorded in my parents' immigration documents" (14, italics in the original). From the start, there is a suspicion and skeptical questioning of the official history that was based on falsified paper work that was a political and social reality for minority groups like the Chinese, the result of subversive attempts to circumnavigate the exclusionary laws. It is also noteworthy that April 20, 1939 was Adolf Hitler's fiftieth birthday, a national holiday in Germany at the time. The occasion came with extravagant demonstrations of the Nazis' military prowess that would soon throw the world into the turmoil of the Second World War, in which China was on the side of the Allies. This political reality of the Second World War would shape Choy's childhood and become a theme in his writing. His childhood includes images of soldiers in Chinatown and stories of past and present racial discrimination. This Chinese Canadian history includes the Chinese Head Tax in the 1890s and "The Day of the Shame," when the Chinese Exclusion Act was passed in 1923, on July 1, ironically also Dominion Day or Canada Day. These ironies and tensions abound in the identity construction of Choy's younger self.

But there are other histories that are more integral to his Chinese Canadian culture and linked to specific expectations. They all feed into his personal history that constructs the identity of this first-person narration, in which the search for identity becomes a search through history. "Think about your Chinese name" (15), his mother tells him: *Way Sun*, a name bestowed by his grandfather, is an old Chinese epigram which means "to rehabilitate" (16), the name itself becoming performative, embodying its future action. In this way, history—both recent and distant—threads itself into Choy's memoir, addressing and rehabilitating the injustices. Choy writes:

> Until after the Second World War, no Chinese, even those born in Canada, like me, were given citizenship: I was a *Resident Alien*, forbidden to vote or to enter any profession, including the law, teaching, medicine and engineering. (74)

There is another historical phenomenon that comes in, more fraught with internal judgement, linked to the bachelor uncles who populate the narrative, who were

> not of the first Chinese who came in the 1850 to pan for gold, but the Chinese who came during the railway and steamship day of British Columbia. Chinatown called them "bachelor men." (72)

The bachelor men are a fringe group within Chinatown culture that the middle-aged narrator seems to identify with, as an unmarried man in his fifties at the time of writing. With a certain playfulness, the memoir calls attention to the blemishes of official history, revealing its unreliability, its tensions and ironies. But there is also an experiential reality, a sensuous experiencing of Chinatown—a spatially lived reality that creates its own memory and truth for the narrator.

Choy grew up in Vancouver's Chinatown, nurtured by its tastes, smells and sounds, and even its ghosts, which breathe life into his literary creations decades later. Chinatown concretizes Choy's childhood experience, not only shaping his own ethnic identity but also birthing his desire—his hunger—to constantly reexamine and reconstitute his identity as a second-generation Chinese Canadian. When asked in an interview if his two novels are *memoir-esque*, Choy answered:

> They are based on my background, and I think I am the kind of writer who is not inventive in the sense of writing sci-fi or writing a story that clearly came out of the imagination. My imagination is connected to my life experience. I'm just that kind of writer. I know it is a limitation, in a way, but also it is not because you are then focused on something you can bring depth to. As I say, I don't know what I know until I write it. (Reed and Choy 2014, 45)

Choy's work records social histories and memories, and it tells stories and creates mythologies bound together through an intimate sense of the Chinatown community and its place in Canada and the wider world.

There occurs a blurring of boundaries between memoir and fiction, which reveal similar preoccupations and themes. In *The Jade Pony* (1995), which won the Trillium Award, being a Chinese in Second World War Vancouver is equated to being an alien. The third brother Sek-Lung (nicknamed Sekky) speaks for many others when he describes his heritage using words that will be echoed in the memoir:

> I was the Canadian-born child of unwanted immigrants who were not allowed to become citizens. The words RESIDENT ALIEN were stamped on my birth certificate, as if I were a loitering stranger. (153)

Likewise, in the Giller Prize finalist *All that Matters* (2004), a novel set during the same era, also in Vancouver, the narrator Kiam-Kim wants to enlist in the Canadian army to fight in the Second World War. But he is discouraged:

> On those documents [such as birth documents and travel certificates] I was designated "Resident Alien." The rumour was that because of our alien status, our yellow skin, and our slanty eyes, the young men of Chinatown would be discouraged from signing up. (285)

Choy's Chinatown childhood memories thread through these works, weaving together a vibrant tapestry out of individual and communal lives, a textured reality of social, economic, and cultural existence infused with a historical awareness.

Writing about "Chineseness" outside of China is not an easy project. The term is fluid, with the different waves of Chinese immigrants coming to Canada and the cross-cultural conversations between new immigrants and the host country. Cultural identities evolve to create hybrid identities when they meet other cultures. In her book, *On Not Speaking Chinese*, Australian critic Ien Ang argues against the hegemonization of Chineseness:

> Chineseness is a category whose meanings are not fixed and pregiven, but constantly renegotiated and rearticulated, both inside and outside China. . . . Diasporas are transnational, spatially and temporally sprawling sociocultural formations of people, creating imagined communities whose blurred and fluctuating boundaries are sustained by real and/or symbolic ties to some original "homeland" . . . It is the myth of the (lost

> or idealized) homeland, the object of both collective memory and of desire and attachment, which is constitutive of diasporas, and which ultimately confines and constrains the nomadism of the diasporic subject. (Ien Ang 2005, 25)

Ang describes the poignant moment when the subject may feel a certain pressure toward a specific diasporic identification with a mythic homeland. She leaves us with a strong sense of the complexities of the Chinese diasporas. Her insights apply to Choy's writing. Being Chinese means to be repeatedly reminded of otherness and not-belonging. But Chineseness was nothing more than a racialized category, and Chinatown is an institutionalized urban space with a strong racial tenor. Consequently, as cultural geographer Kay J Anderson sums it up, the concept of Chinatown is more than the physical location of a community, and it is an idea that "has been a critical nexus through which the race definition process was structured" (Anderson 1987, 580).

Paper Shadows offers a cartographical representation of Vancouver's Chinatown that spatializes the everyday activities of its dwellers, facilitating a reimagining of an active and lively community that fosters multicultural development in Vancouver. In this sense, through his childhood memory of the 1940s—Chinese opera, food, festivals, and family relations—Choy transforms a static, institutionalized, and racialized urban space into a dynamic, individualized and vibrant cultural space. French cultural theorist Michel de Certeau used the term "spatial stories" to emphasize the interdependency of textual narratives and spatial practices. When people move through urban space, they craft individualized histories infused with personal meanings. Choy's unique way of navigating Chinatown creates a literary itinerary as spatial practice. For de Certeau, a place is "an instantaneous configuration of positions," and thus entails "an indication of stability" (de Certeau 2011, 117). If Chinatown is merely perceived as an urban physical place, it falls into the racialization of the community. However, Choy mobilizes the idea of Chinatown as cultural space, which is created by the practices of the community. "Space is a practiced place," de Certeau adds (117). By composing stories about Chinatown and its residents, Choy tactically reconstructs the public image of Chinatown, transforming the victimized urban community into a historical subject, an attempt at an honest and unadulterated retelling of history, while also composing his younger self. These kinds of stories, in de Certeau's words, "carry out a labor that constantly transforms places into spaces or spaces into places" (118). Thus, Chinatown becomes the "practiced place" which embodies the landscape of Chinese ethnic history in exile and also an important cultural legacy in Canada's multicultural history.

In *Paper Shadows*, we discern many ironic layers as Choy composes his self-portraits, snippets of images and memories that create the identity which is never stable or fully defined but always reveals tensions and fractures. While the characters in his novels are uniquely different in life experience and self-realization, they all mimic Choy's self-presentation in his memoir, and perhaps this gives him different possibilities to unfold his Chinatown years. Choy speaks and deals in a language that has become accessible to members outside the Chinatown community. Through the spatial stories of Chinatown, Choy tactically negotiates his identity within the larger domain of coastal space in Vancouver.

On the surface, Choy appears to be raised with a different culture and mindset in an exclusive community that was Vancouver's Chinatown. Chinese culture appears prominently throughout Choy's upbringing, and his surroundings seem to hold on to Chinese culture with regards to food, entertainment, beliefs, and other everyday practices. However, it is too simplistic to read Choy's work as the typical diasporic "unbelonging"—neither here nor there, or Canada as the unhomely new home and old China as the far-away longed-for home. For Choy, Chinatown is his belonging and longing, and his writing radiates his cultural commitment to this special community. He complicates and intervenes the so-called second-generation struggles in identity negotiation and cultural belonging, and demonstrates that Chinatown is an important part of Vancouver's multicultural growth. He writes:

> My English, however, centered around the boyish images of Hollywood. Nothing Chinese could save me. I saw cowboys everywhere. I collected cowboy comics. And when I chose a bedtime book, it was always an English-language book, and some of my babysitters even read them aloud to me . . . Soon,

> Chinatown began to fade, like a ghost. I was turning into a banana: yellow on the outside and white on the inside. (84)

Being a "banana" indicates "a reductionist attitude to issues of culture, community, and race" (Khoo 2003, 1). It implies that one cannot be Chinese and Canadian simultaneously and that being a Chinese in multicultural Canada means being positioned in an in-between space: not really excluded but also not fully included. Choy confronts his identity-changing alongside Chinatown's "fade." His literary tactics remind us of Lisa Lowe's critical interrogation of ethnic subjectivity in diasporic culture. Lowe argues that "the processes that produce such identity are never complete and are always constituted in relation to historical and material difference" (Lowe 1996, 64). In this way, Choy questions simple and closed understandings about what it means to be Chinese in Canada, and he turns Chinatown into a liminal space for diversity development and possible different self-realizations especially for a second-generation Chinese immigrant.

When his family moves to their new house on Keefer Street, little Choy feels that there is a ghost living with them due to the recurring noises of nighttime. And they call that ghost *bak kwei*, "a white man's ghost" (*Paper Shadows* 32). This concept suggests something of the Chinatown people's precarious existence during war time, their alienated and marginalized status within the large white hegemony of Vancouver's cityscape. When Choy revisits those childhood ghost memories with his mother in his twenties, the two of them logically conclude that it is because "Vancouver is located on a fault line. The earth moves. The noise was the house settling, the foundation shifting" (33). This spatial instability, however, reflected the ever-evolving definition of Chineseness for the diasporic community. In addition, Choy is masterful in capturing the unique weathered look and moody climate of the coastal city. Likewise, in the novel *The Jade Peony*, Sekky's older sister Jook-Liang says, "The spring sun overhead reminded me it was nearing twelve o'clock: the mill whistle by the BC docks would bellow soon. The air felt wet and warm, spring and summer, though it was mid-spring. Small clouds scudded cross the mountain tops" (*The Jade Peony* 44).

The location of Vancouver on the costal land does not only bring nighttime noises and weathered looks, but also a particular historical social circumstance during the Second World War, when the Canadian military were omnipresent and the *Chinese Times* was filled with maps of Europe and Asia. Chinatown was a site of tourism, a "safe terrain in which to spend the extra wartime dollars pouring into West Coast port cities such as Vancouver" (*Paper Shadows* 69). Chinatown had come a long way from the impoverished place of the 1930s, undesirable for tourists. By wartime, Chinatown was known for its "exotic" goods:

> The military men who walked through Chinatown were mainly Caucasian sailors and soldiers, tall as giants. The city of Vancouver, with its crowded railway stations and packed harbours, was the last stop before soldiers and sailors shipped out; and the perfumed and powdered ladies from the back rooms of Gastown hotels and bars made Chinatown a favourite place to take shore leave . . . Once, while Mother was negotiating the price of a rare pair of stockings, I remember, a soldier pushed through the busy aisles of Kuo Kong Silk to outbid her. (67)

While tourists flocked to Chinatown for an authentic experience, young Wayson Choy made his own discovery, namely, the cowboys of East Hastings disappearing behind entrances marked "Men Only." The photograph that illustrates this chapter is of Choy as a boy on a bucking horse—a scene staged for the camera—having fun at the Pacific National Exhibition, waving his hand, a smile planted on his face. Far from presenting a static, romanticized image and memory of Chinatown's community, the narrative highlights its transformation and flux. This is not the space where he could enjoy the fantasy of an authentic Chinese cultural experience, purely owned by its community members. It shows that the harmonious multicultural society is a myth, as is the precondition of race as an indicator of cultural difference and the idea of Canada as a white nation.

For Choy, the coastal space of Vancouver is a social space, where physical space interacts with symbolic space. Or to put it into Henri Lefebvre's words, social space "subsumes things produced, and encompasses their interrelationships in their co-existence and simultaneity—their (relative) order and/or (relative) disorder" (73). Thus, the coastal space is an example of such a social space, where the particular location brings its own cultural history. It is not only the mediator of geographical relationships, but also the process of an embodiment of experience. In Choy's case, Chinatown is turned into a new idea, which is negotiated but unsettled, requiring a continual, yet uncomfortable, shift in identities, confronting the space also with a sense of loss. Engaging with the past and integrating it into both Chinatown and his own identity, Choy inspires a theorization of the coastal space by exploring the locality of ethnic history. Choy's writing about Vancouver's Chinatown performs coastal space as ethnic history, and offers a central consideration of generative coastal aesthetics in Canadian literature. Choy has delineated the multiple and dovetailing effects of Vancouver's coastal space on individuals and the community.

In a 1999 interview, Choy explains his intention to write about Vancouver's old Chinatown, and insists that "I want to understand the horrible times my parents and the pioneer generation went through, and why and how they were able to survive at all" (Deer and Choy 1999, 41). Chinatown provides Choy with both a material and a symbolic locus from which to retell the stories of his families and reclaim the histories of Vancouver's Chinatown as a community member and as someone who personally experienced the history and the space. In his study of Choy's novel, Christopher Lee maintains that "Chinese Canadians continued to uphold the family as survival strategy" (Lee 1999, 21). I want to emphasize that Choy's writings create a public consciousness that can be galvanized on behalf of the embattled Chinatown community under the large social and political anti-alterity. As a Chinatown resident, as a survivor of the community going through dark times, and as the child of those Chinatown survivors who went through the discriminatory political act and the social exclusion of the Chinese, Choy guides us into a historical ecosystem, and imagines the possibilities for cultural reconciliation. Choy continues in the interview, "Chinatown was not a community of victims. There were the racist attitudes towards the sexual activities of a people who were told they had no more right to life than animals. They surmounted all of that, those who did survive" (41).

Choy's writing style may be described as anti-epic. There is no single elevated and superior hero-character in his writings. Nor do Choy's real and imagined characters dominate their environments; they are firmly enmeshed within the contingencies of their surroundings and their heritage. Nor are they assigned to have a teleological destination—they are always evolving and adapting, just as Chinatown itself does over years and decades of family history. Choy's creative works present a sensitive account of his own experience as a Canada-born Chinese Canadian and unfold the various ways of renegotiating one's identities. As Choy says: "one lives one's life in moments, not in the grand sweep of plotline" (41). This fragmentary narration of moments is also a quintessential part of his postmodern style.

Reading Choy's Chinatown does more than illuminate the voyage of Chinese immigration to Canada or Chinese diasporic culture. It takes readers inside the dynamic of Chinese Canadian identity construction, using postmodernist literary devices to do so, confronting us with both the opportunities and limitations of documentary paper evidence. In the process, his work is fundamental to understanding the racialized foundations of both the immigration acts of Canada and Canadian multiculturalism. He grapples with the issues of immigrant family history within the community of Vancouver's Chinatown; at the same time, his works rupture the conventional understanding of the Chinese diaspora and Chinatown culture in Canada. He debunks the stereotype of a victimized minority culture and defies the fetishization of the exotic urban space for the purpose of white consumption; simultaneously he reconstructs the space by using the trope of the coastal landscape—the space between land and sea—to reimagine a cultural integration with the large urban community in Vancouver.

By the time his second memoir *Not Yet: A Memoir of Living and Almost Dying* was published in 2009, Choy had long left Vancouver and made Toronto his habitat. The recent book focuses on his Toronto years and tells the story of the heart and asthma attacks that almost killed him. Vancouver's Chinatown, and his childhood in that community, still linger on in his mind. Waking up in the hospital bed, his physical movements limited, Choy's semiconsciousness returns him to the spatial wandering through Chinatown. He writes,

> All I knew for sure was that I was still in a hospital, caught in a catastrophe, and that someone was standing by me. Yet voices faintly echoed from my past, the nagging warnings of parents and the elders of Chinatown, their fears for my bachelor ways singsonged back into my drugged head like a chorus from an ancient opera. (10)

Chinatown continues to play an essential part in Choy's literary career, and carries significant implications for his own understanding of his past, his self, and his community. Choy's words are telling, as he writes: "my mother and father and the community of Vancouver's Chinatown had nurtured my in-between generation" (138). The voices of parents and elders are still his cultural guide—but also his cultural superego, nagging when he fails to meet the ideal. These voices remind readers of the cross-generational and cross-textual legacy that threads through his entire oeuvre; they remind us of the narrator's relentless efforts at integrating and readapting the cultural fragments of his identity. In this, the arc of Choy's name, Way Sun, and its formidable powers to rehabilitate and restore have come full circle, back to the beginning.

RAMABAI ESPINET

Landscape and Diasporic Citizenship(s) in Ramabai Espinet's *The Swinging Bridge* and *Nuclear Seasons*[1]

Dannabang Kuwabong

> It turned out that the land rumours were true. Kello had been negotiating to buy back Pappy's land in Trinidad. The whole property, he said, the land on Manahambre Road, with Pappy and Mama's house on the Pierre Street end and our big wooden structure smack in the middle. My memories on the train about this early childhood home of ours came back sharply.

The subject of this conversation between the dying Kello and his sister Mona in *The Swinging Bridge* (2003, 53) has often been overlooked as the central theme of Ramabai Espinet's work; critics have focused instead on gender, historical, and cultural themes. Yet issues of land/landscape/place/home occur throughout her work. In this essay, I explore how this Indo-Trinidadian Canadian writer engages the issues of land/landscape/place in two of her works: The novel, *The Swinging Bridge*, and the poetry collection, *Nuclear Seasons* (1991). My point of departure recognizes that Canadian writers who emigrated from the Caribbean, Africa, and Asia expand the Canadian literary landscape because their literary output draw on memories of other cultural, historical, and physical landscapes that are not traditionally or historically Canadian. These other landscapes support the imagined policy of inclusiveness in Canada's multicultural ideal. They open the literary and cultural borders that have remained well-guarded by the assumption that Canada's literary landscape must reflect European Canadian constructs.

It is legitimate to consider the literary products of these new Canadians from their own cultural, historical, and linguistic paradigms and not to sweep them under the rubric used to study Canadian canonical texts. Ramabai Espinet's work is hence to be responded to through her Indo-Trinidadian Canadian consciousness. As an exile who finds a homeplace in Canada but refuses to disaffiliate herself from her Indo-Trinidadian culture and history, her position in effect reflects the observations of Edward Said: "The exile knows that in a secular and contingent world, homes are always provisional. Borders and barriers which enclose us within the safety of familiar territory can also become prisons, and are often defended beyond reason or necessity. Exiles cross borders, break barriers of thought and experience" (Said 1990, 365). Said's idea of the provisionality of a homeplace for the exile is echoed by Stuart Hall's idea of a "one-way trip" (Hall 1987, 44) without guaranteeing a place "to go back to" (44). Espinet has articulated this concept in her theory of "nowarianism" or what other Caribbean diaspora writers call "wayfarianism." This mode of thinking had earlier been voiced by Heidegger: "Homelessness is coming to be the destiny of the world" (2008, 219). Nowarian consciousness derives from the nomadic lives of Caribbean peoples as conceptualized in Edouard Glissant's *Poetics of Relations* (1997), but it is not an absence of a consciousness of place or home, and memories of lands and landscapes that shape the diasporic life. Rather, it is akin to a type of circular nomadism that Glissant posits as a trademark of Antilleans.

Glissant asserts that the metamorphic changes experienced by enslaved Africans and indentured Asians in the Caribbean initiate a new concept of place/landscape/home/origins. He writes: "their ordeal did not die; it quickened into this continuous/discontinuous thing: see panic of the new land, the haunting of the former land, finally the alliance with the imposed land, suffered and redeemed" (11). Glissant's elements of metamorphic changes then provide the conceptual framework with which to define and understand Espinet's nowarian ideology. Nowarian consciousness reflects the "notion of the rhizome . . . the idea of a rootedness [which simultaneously] challenges that of a totalitarian root" (11). Rootless rootedness is also defined as errantry and exile in tangential relationships that ontologize Antillean diasporicity and/or deterritorialized identities. Errantry "silently emerges from the deconstructing of compact national entities that yesterday were still triumphant and, at the same time, from different, uncertain births of new forms of identity that call to us" (18). In situations of errantry, as related to Caribbean peoples, "uprooting can work toward identity, and exile can be seen as . . . a search for the Other (through circular nomadism) rather than as an expansion of territory (an arrowlike nomadism)" (18).

Nomadicity or nowarianism, does not translate into a "renunciation" of Trinidadian or Indian places and landscapes. It however suggests levels of frustration regarding "deteriorated situation[s] of origin; it is not a resolute act of rejection or an uncontrolled impulse of abandonment" (18). Thus, Indo-Caribbean Canadian "identity is no longer completely within the [totalitarian and/or territoriality] root [traceable to India or Trinidad] but [exists] also in Relation" to [Canada] (18). As an Indo-Trinidadian English-speaking Protestant-Presbyterian new Canadian, Espinet engages her nowarian consciousness to understand, appropriate, and enter Quebec, Canada's French-speaking space besieged by English-speaking Canada. Espinet, through Mona, is aware that "[i]n the pursuit of [her] desires across such frontiers [she is] paradoxically forced to face [her] confines, together with that excess that seeks to sustain the dialogues across them. Transported some way into the border country, [she] observe[s] the possibility of another place, another world, another future" (Chambers 5). Mona states this struggle in these words: "Mona Singh. That's me. I live in the eye of a storm. My whole life arches backwards and forwards according to the speed of the guts around me. In the centre, near the eye, in the place where I live, it is still" (*The Swinging Bridge* 5). Using hurricane imagery associated with her Trinidadian landscape, she draws attention to the struggles against definitions that limit her.

My idea of landscape as articulated in Espinet's poetry and fiction is further informed by postcolonial notions such as the "complex interaction of language, history and environment. It is characterised firstly by a sense of displacement in those who moved to the colonies, . . . a gap between the 'experienced' environment and the descriptions the language provides . . . and by the immense investment of culture in the construction of place" (Ashcroft, Griffiths, and Tiffin 391). Place, accordingly, generates "creative tension[s] between language and the sense of dislocation from an historical 'homeland' and that created by the dissonance between language, the experience of 'displacement'" (391). Consequently, *The Swinging Bridge*, as a "postcolonial text . . . [is a] metonym of the continual process of reclamation" of Indo-Trinidadian Canadian cultural realities. A place understood as "a palimpsest, a kind of parchment on which successive generations have inscribed and rein-scribe the process of history" (392) provides the critical scaffolding from which I construct my reading of Espinet's work as a tensional relationship between the natural or city spaces of Trinidad and Canada and their influences on their human inhabitants.

These preliminary detours facilitate my prognosis of how Trinidadian place/landscape/ecology acts as the "central figurative tool for situating [Indo-Caribbean-Canadian] identity[ies], history[ies] and cultural memory[ies]" (Tolia-Kelly 57), while exploring "the role and value of *landscape* to [Indo-Trinidad's] mobile diasporic communities" (57). In addition, I endorse her argument that the "myriad of landscapes" (57) experienced by diasporic groups enable them to construct new citizenships and identities through mapped "connections to past landscapes . . . " In Espinet's novel, Kello's act of buying back the lost family land in Trinidad starts as a business venture even if later it translates into a project of restoration of family name: "'Mona,' he said, and his tone was sharp, 'I want you to go and act on my behalf. Go to Trinidad, inspect the land, and confirm that the transaction takes place . . . Bess says that the whole Southland is booming because of oil revenues. She is suggesting a development—terraced townhouses . . . I'm asking you to go look at the property, get a feel for things'" (*The Swinging Bridge* 53). Mona responds differently to this commission. Not fully grasping Kello's intent, she dreams of reliving her childhood memories in this place that she thought had been erased: "My memories on the train about this early childhood home of ours came back sharply" (*The Swinging Bridge* 53). The mention of the land, triggers Mona's emotional and historical connections with this landscape. Consequently, when she returns with the title deed, it uncovers the historical links of the property to three generations of her family. Thus, apart from it being a good business venture, Kello's repurchase of the land is liberatory. It restores the lost family prestige and name, and erases Da-Da's guilt for gambling away the land. Nevertheless, this act does disaffiliate the family from the Canadian landscape. Canada provided the landscape and place for Kello's success, and becomes the place of his death.

I adopt Paul Carter's call to "develop a framework of [reading] that makes the [New Canadian] central, not ancillary, to [Canadian] historical processes" (7). The "discursive formations of power" (Brah 125) within a camouflaged rigid Canadian literary landscape is counterbalanced by Espinet's memories of Indo-Trinidadian cultural and historical places. Solbaic asserts, "Landscape, whether as a geographical space or imaginary reconstruction of place memory, contains the cultural spirit that enables Indo-Trinidadians to carry an indomitable cultural identity in Canada, while allowing for a selective embrace of aspects of Canadian multiculturalism" (Solbaic 230). Embracing Canada's literary multiculturalism reveals, as Brah insinuates, "no single overarching locus of power where dominance, subordination, solidarity, and affiliation based on egalitarian principles, or the conditions of affinity, conviviality and sociality are produced and secured, once and for all" (125). Thus, when Mona insists that she lives in the eye of the storm (*The Swinging Bridge* 5), she refers "to the variety of ways specific [Canadian literary] discourses of differences are constituted, reproduced, or reassigned" (Solbaic 125-126), and used to either validate or invalidate and canonize or ignore Indo-Caribbean-Canadian texts. Her defiance of such discursive power relations is reflected in her response to the Montreal landscape and weather in November: "It is late November and the Montreal city streets are slick with freezing rain when I return. I hunch my shoulders and walk faster. My walk is purposeful and strong. The chill in the air is pungent, the leaves have fallen, the year is coming to a close. I am part of this city I live in, and right now I want no other place" (*The Swinging Bridge* 305). And, "Like any other migrant navigating new terrain, I bring my own beat to the land around me . . . Any new beat is like that: parts of it at war with itself until the separate parts recognize the point of fusion and merge seamlessly. When the rhythm becomes right, everyone forgets the time when cacophony threatened to drown the whole enterprise" (305).

Thus, for Mona, "Boundaries between groups [are] signified as inherently different . . . [yet] relational, contingent and variable" (Solbaic 126). Both *The Swinging Bridge* and *Nuclear Seasons* challenge yet endorse, "collective, historical, political, [economic, cultural, familial, gendered, religious and personal] experience[s] [that] . . . interrogate and challenge essentialist constructions of group boundaries" (126) normalized in Canadian literary studies. Espinet consciously writes from a revisionary standpoint of history and culture that both claims yet critiques aspects of a misguided racist ideology that believes that "It's Indian time now" (*The Swinging Bridge* 300) in Trinidad after years of Afro-Trinidadian hegemony.

Place as landscape, as expressed through Mona, Kello, Horatio, Da-Da, and Babsie in the novel, "is a mythic place of desire in the diasporic imagination . . . a place of no return, even if possible to visit the place of 'origin' . . . home is also the lived experience of a locality. Its sounds and smells, its heat and dust, balmy summer evenings, or the excitement of the first snowfall, shivering winter evenings . . . " (Brah 192) Brah's "concept of diaspora" as "places [where] the discourse of 'home' and 'dispersion' [are] in creative tension, inserting a homing desire while simultaneously critiquing discourses of fixed origins" (193), is applicable to Espinet's work. Of course, Brah is aware that for writers such as Espinet, the "problematic of 'home' belonging may be integral to [her] diasporic condition, but how, when, and in what form questions surface, or how they are addressed, is specific to the history of [her] particular diaspora" (193). He, however, misjudges how Indo-Trinidadian Canadians define their "home." He writes: "for South Asian groups in Trinidad, cultural identification with the Asian subcontinent might be the most important element" (193). By downplaying the overwhelming evidence pointing to Trinidad as the desired homeplace among Indo-Trinidadians, rather than Asia-India, Brah lumps all Indian-Canadians together without any differentiations. Yes, Asia-India is indeed an important symbolic imaginary homeplace for the Indian diaspora, but for Indo-Trinidadians, Trinidad is the paramount geographical landscape of desire, it is the place that birthed their present families; a place to (re)visit, (re)settle, and (re)claim.

Mona does not mince words when she asserts that Trinidad is where her family's roots are, and that it is from Trinidad that the family has carved new routes to new lands: "For generations the members of our family had all come to consciousness . . . rooted to the same spot on the island, seeing the same trees and streams and beaches, bound by the same loss; then, in my generation, everything had changed" (*The Swinging Bridge* 151). Her lament about how the loss of place and subsequent dispersal of the family from Trinidad, results in "Kello . . . dying among strangers, with only a few family members around him" and "Esau [his best friend living] in an English suburb and they had not seen each other for years" (151). Mona may believe that "earlier in life, Kello had not set himself the task of buying back the land in Manahambre Road" (161), but in providing the money to buy back the land as a business venture, Kello provides the family with the possibility of going "back in the same house, the ancestral lands reclaimed. I was sure a deeper meaning would unravel in time, but for now I felt as if our history was like a spider's web in which we were all caught fast" (161). Kello's power of reclaiming his ancestral landscape, Ogborn argues (104), is an act of reconstructed "geographies" of historical, cultural, and gender homes (Tolia-Kelly 117), where "[l]andscapes . . . are valued as formal iconographies of past citizenries" (117) and past intra-island migrations.

Trinidad evokes happy memories of grandpa, grandma, cane fields, nature's scents and smells, the songs of Baboonie, etc., in a bucolic life of freedom with securer agency and sense of personhood: "I imagined Pappy setting out alone in the cool of the night, the high whitemoon riding in the western sky, directly over the Gulf of Paria . . . Pappy picking his way through Corinth, Cocoyea, already smelling of coffee boiling in coal pots at the roadside by the time he reached Petitbourg . . . with tall canes on both sides" (269). However, it would be misleading to assert that this is all that Trinidad evokes in Mona. There are also the memories of the Afro-Trinidadian and Indo-Trinidadian divide, British colonial education, Canadian Presbyterian evangelism, and the dysfunctional aspects of her extended family. Intra-Trinidadian landscapes are Espinet's canvases that secure spatial and temporal narrative demarcations for (re)negotiating her story. Temporal spatiality, Tolia-Kelly observes, is the "dialectical relationship between memory and *placing* [which] is critical for diasporic [Indo-Trinidadian Canadians] who have migrated through varied landscapes, but who have also varied political connections with territory and national [and linguistic, cultural, historical, and religious] identities" (75). Therefore, to read Espinet is to enter Mona's, Kello's, Babsie's, Muddie's, and even Da-Da's Indo-Trinidadian Canadian socio-political and multicultural matrixes consisting of their complex, interconnected lives with their individual and collective senses of "place, natures and landscape" (75).

In *Nuclear Seasons*, the poet renders no apologies when she claims this about Trinidad: "This land is home to me," (10) because her memories recollect the landscape ecologies and place events like "Hosay Nights" (9-10), when the child recalls the loneliness, poverty, and misery of indentured ancestors in Trinidad; the hard work of the indentured Indian woman in the cane fields in Trinidad in "Tamani: a cane-cutting woman," the mother who rose at dawn "to her blackening footsteps / . . . / At twilight she stood alone / Her shining cutlass green with grass" (11). In several poems, Espinet recaptures the landscape of her childhood and teenage years that provided her a sense of place, a home, which is not India, as in V S Naipaul's *The Mimic Men*. To Espinet, the India of "Sadhu days and babu days / And Mai in Ohmi days" are lost to her like " . . . elephants / And silks, the dhows of Naipaul's / Yearning, not mine" (10). Unlike Naipaul's hopes, "to give expression to the restlessness, the deep disorder, which the great explorations, the overthrow in three continents of established social organization, the unnatural bringing together of peoples who could achieve fulfillment only within the security of their own societies and the landscape" (*The Mimic Men* 38), Espinet rejects the call "to give partial expression to the restlessness which this great upheaval has brought about" (38). She argues in "A Nowhere Place" (*Nuclear Seasons* 37) that her love is for a "nowhere space, / An angled, un-collared striding land, / The only place to live" (37). Moreover, she claims to be "much too much a victim of that restlessness which was to have been my subject" (*The Mimic Men* 38) to become a spokesperson for Indo-Caribbean Canadian peoples.

Refusing this mantle of spokesperson for global-Indianness, Espinet claims instead an Antillean Canadian space, not as disaffiliation with India but as assertion of her new roots. That rootedness in Trinidad, the result of forced migration and settlement, generates greater feelings of affiliation and entitlement. Without question, Espinet laments the consequences of the forced migration of Indians to Trinidad, and the nomadic life it subsequently initiated, which has made them, "Now homeless, a true refugee / Of the soul's last corner" (10). She pictorializes Trinidad through the imageries of fishing activities, carnival, flora and fauna, agriculture, deaths and births. These images are accentuated in "An Ageable Woman" (81-83), who worked Trinidad's soil, lived its histories, and welcomes the emerging cultural changes associated with the youth. Espinet recognizes her Indian origins, for example in "Lost Cargoes" (84-87), but they are conceived in an imaginary and mythical past contaminated during the crossing of the Kalipani.

In contrast, in *The Swinging Bridge* Uncle Baddall aka Ralph, Horatio's father, constructs a false history that romanticizes the Indo-Trinidadian past (226-229). He leaves Horatio with a pile of useless maps and notes purporting to contain secrets of a treasure buried by some imaginary royalty who fled India to Trinidad. This depiction is clearly the author's critique of revisionary histories by Indo-Trinidadians that are blatantly false. Indians in Trinidad, Mona explains, "were bent on creating fortunes out of nothing—that was what they considered their genius. That nothing was us, flung by one turn of the wheel of fortune into a place entirely unknown, where we built our lives not out of nothing, but out of the lack of the back-breaking work of reinvention" (303). To gloss over the history of the initial horrors of the (forced or otherwise) Indian migrations to Trinidad, with false promises of new beginnings, is simply irresponsible. Nonetheless, the impact of that history on Indo-Caribbeans is their propensity to migrate: "If you happen to be born into an Indian family, an Indian family from the Caribbean, migratory, never certain of the terrain, that's how life falls down around you. . . . The outside encroaches, but the ramparts are strong, and once you leave it you have no shelter and no ready skills for finding a different one. I found that out after years of trying" (15).

Landscape as place, therefore, in *The Swinging Bridge* and *Nuclear Seasons*, transcends mapped physical reliefs to include "texture, colour, and smells of soils" (Tolia-Kelly 77) that Mona recollects. "Bree and Me" (16-17), "Forest Flower" (18), "Rain Time" (19-20), and "A Fishing Song" (23-24) testify in favor of her inseparable bonding with her Trinidad. As she confesses, "The first thing I wanted to do was to visit the land. Kello had been right, I thought. Buying the land had brought him and Pappy together again. Pappy had been right too, holding on to the land and warning Da-Da not to throw it away" (268). Canada's landscape lacks similar social and emotional warmth. To Mona there is an incongruity between the "quiet treelined street in downtown Toronto" (54) and the disguised racism of the European Canadian neighbors: "The neighbourhood conveyed an atmosphere of settled values, Victorian chic, and elaborately concealed Anglo-Saxon attitudes. I'm not fooled by all of this fake gentility" (54). Mona then reveals a similar feeling in Montreal. As she walks along Sherbrooke Street, she has an epiphany in the way she now relates to the Montreal landscape: "Something . . . cracked inside me. I felt it, although I had no ready explanation. Something had brought my drifting lifestyle to an end. But I resisted it. Montreal had provided me with a charmed space where I could live free of commitment. I was neither Québécoise nor Anglo; I had felt no passion about Quebec's future in Canada" (242). She now feels "[n]othing . . . [about Montreal or Quebec] anymore. I walked through those streets I had grown to love, thinking of my early years here, of the friends and lovers of that time, the nights spent drinking and arguing at the Swiss Hut" (242). In contrast, Trinidad's landscape unpacks childhood remembrances laced with the intimate stories of family and community. "It is true that navel strings mean something. Tiny Daisy's navel string under the caimite tree in Iere Village is marked by a yellow croton bush, planted by Grandma Lil so many years ago to mark the birth and death of her firstborn. All our navel strings are buried in the Manahambre land. I remember Da-Da digging the hole . . . " (77-78) The trauma of failure experienced by Da-Da, which compelled him to emigrate to Canada, can now be healed through an apologetic explanation: "Da-Da did not like the idea of migrating and starting all over, but in the end he decided to leave [for Canada], even though it meant that his separation from the earth that had made him, the earth where his navel string was buried, was now complete" (77).

Thus, Kello's act of rebuying the land, though guided by business interests, nonetheless sets the process for the redemption of family name, and the reunification with Trinidad as a place of rebirth and returns, without foreclosing their spaces/places within the Canadian landscape. It is the Canadian landscape itself that enables them to shift back and forth "in relation to this process of the presencing of these physical memories" of Trinidad (Tolia-Kelly 78). These memories, compounded by the ghosts of India encapsulated in Baboonie's songs and Grandma Lil's notes about Great-grandma Gainder's journey across the Kalipani from India, converge to create for Mona a mental space of her own in which to negotiate her shifting and hybridized terrains. These shifting terrains are, "points of resistance to exclusive dominant [Euro-Canadian] cultures as well as . . . points of engagement to an enfranchising ideal located in the [Indian past]" (79) and the Trinidadian present dominated by Afro-Trinidadian nationalist and racialized discourses (70-76), which Mona aggregates to her benefit.

This aggregation of multiple experiences of dislocations and relocations, disaffiliations and reaffiliations, with Trinidad and Canada (Tolia-Kelly 11), become construction material for her transnational Indo-Trinidadian Canadian identity. She recreates and develops her Indo-Trinidadian Canadian citizenship(s) in symbiotic, syncretic, and transgressive relationships across the different landscapes. This process begins after she has an epiphany following her initial trip to Trinidad to carry out Kello's wishes. It is expressed in the sudden public exposure of her masquerade aimed at achieving invisibility in Montreal (*The Swinging Bridge* 242). She had believed that "Montreal had provided [her] with a charmed space where [she] could live free of commitment" as she was "neither Québécoise nor Anglo . . . my very anonymity offered a kind of freedom difficult to imagine anywhere else. If I left Montreal, I feared that my shell would dissolve, leaving me naked, bare for all the world to see" (242). An old man in Montreal strips her of that illusion. This awakening enables her to ask herself: "Was [the old man] struck by something, the naked want on my face maybe?" (242) Mona's shame of her unveiling is intensified by her recall of Da-Da's first encounter with the landscape of Toronto: "When I arrived in the early seventies, Canada was a white country . . . For Da-Da, the moment of truth came when he saw a wall covered with graffiti that read Keep Canada White . . . [and] that first year winter piled up in huge drifts around me," and she realized that Canada promised an illusion of freedom that only translated into being "set adrift . . . [with] no course mapped out for me" (242-243). In comparison, Trinidad provides a grounding in cartographic details, scripted on the deed of the land.

San Fernando's landscape remains indelible in her memory: "So many, many years have passed and yet I know it well, the rise of land from Cedar Hill curving upwards to Hope Road and then down the hill again, bending twice into looping hairpin curves before stretching out to a semicircle around our land, then rising up again, gently now, to Pierre Street" (120). This is the land of her beginnings, "the land where Da-Da had brought Muddie as a bride" (120). Indeed, Mona gives topographic details of the land, its vegetation, cane fields, and rivers, making emotional connections to her childhood. The landscape yields half-forgotten memories of love between Mona and Da-Da: "The hill at the top of the land is broad and wide, just as it always was, but now spreading below is a forested wilderness, unfamiliar in shape, thick with unknown shrubs and trees. I wonder about snakes as I work my way through the bush, but Pappy's voice is loud and clear rising from the pit where he used to roast sweet potatoes for us . . . " (121) The Trinidadian landscape implies a type of independence that Canada does not guarantee: "Pappy would dig the red sweet potatoes out of the fresh dirt and scrub them clean, then pierce them with an iron stake he rotated for hours above the fire. It was an ingenious little contraption, like the others he made, my old grandfather: the file for his papers and bills, which was the end of an old coat hanger" (121). The euphoric details of the natural environment bring out memories of the past: "In my memory the chenette tree comes first, then the chataigne tree at the side, and the giant breadfruit tree just beyond. Finally the zaboca tree and the cluster of three mammy-sepote tress, close to the sweet potato pit" (121).

The map of the purchased land that Mona brings back to Toronto signals a transplantation of memories of Trinidad onto the liminal spaces of Canada, and moves Babsie, "to tears at the sight of the place where she was born, the landscape that had no presence in her memories" (149). The map, a document with coded entitlement, facilitates the Indo-Trinidadian insertion of their cultural, ecological, and historical landscapes into Canada's landscapes. It generates an acceptance that identities are defined by multiple transitional landscapes. Canada provides a deterritorialized consciousness, while Trinidad secures for a sense of reterritorialization. As Rob Nixon has argued, "distance from any clear-cut national identity or notion of home" land (3), reflected in the multiple territorialities in *The Swinging Bridge*, underpin Espinet's concept of Indo-Trinidadian Canadian subjectivities from multidimensional spaces.

Trinidad convokes and evokes a landscape of rootedness, a place where the horrors of Indian indenture, humiliation, conversion to Christianity, converge and generate spaces for self-identification. Mona's emotional and devotional reverence for the land, now that it is a place where the family can reunite, gives her courage to fight the emptiness of anonymity in Montreal: "I walk around the land . . . recalling where the chenette and celamen and breadfruit trees had stood. I imagine that something of me, and of all our lives here, lies buried in it. I sit on the ground and then lie flat. I press my face into the earth and search for my scent" (270). Her desire to corporeally merge with the soil of the land of her birth triggers the smells of nature that her life in Montreal could not erase. The "musky, wild scent like that of a young child, running all day through the land, between trees and bushes, lying on dirt, . . . and then, . . . just before darkness hits . . . they call her inside to bathe quickly, washing the dirt off her feet at the standpipe outside . . . before they soap the smell off her . . . " (270) Mona is ecstatic. She derives emotional and spiritual security from this brief yet lasting corporeal bonding with Trinidad's natural environment. She writes: "And I was not disappointed. The smell I had then rose up into my nostrils from the land, up from long ago. The land, the land had remembered. I lay face down on the earth, my first earth, breathing it" (270). This "creative reconstruction of the lived environment, the reassertion of place in language and textuality" is Mona's "key to a deep-seated cultural transformation" (Ashcroft 124). Thus, Mona demonstrates that for Indo-Trinidadian Canadians, identities are constructed through "[p]lace, and the experience of displacement, emerge out of the infection of a language, history, visual perception, spatiality and environment" (125).

However, this does not elide the reality of Trinidad's ethnic and racial tensions that block Indo-Caribbean people's full participation in the cultural politics of newly independent Trinidad. These tensions act as the catalysts for Da-Da's decision to emigrate to Canada. Migration to Da-Da and other Indo-Trinidadians in the 1960s was "a learned adaptive response to changing individual and environmental circumstances, to search for better opportunities . . . Both internal . . . and international migration . . . are potential responses to conditions at home in comparison to conditions elsewhere" (Conway 148). For Da-Da, the pressure to migrate to a new place is "[a] response to political turmoil [and] economic pressure (especially impoverishment)" (148). His decision to relocate originates in his feeling of internal dislocation on the land of his birth, and his departure to Canada becomes his "survival strategy" as he feels "underprivileged" as an Indo-Trinidadian in the new Trinidad (148). Economic reasons also influence Da-Da's decision to relocate to Canada. Guilty that he lost Pappy's and Mama's land through gambling debts, he looks for excuses: "I was at the lowest point of my life. The old people sweat blood to buy the land and to keep it through thick and thin. For me, for us, for all of you . . . But God turn his back on me, he turn me into his stepchild . . . I was sucking salt day and night for so long I forget any other way to live" (150). Da-Da penitential lament is exacerbated by an overwhelming guilt toward "those two old people [who] knew that they had to keep the land. I knew that too—I always knew that. And I try, I really try, but the time was different" (150). Kello's reclamation of his ancestral land in Trinidad, taxonomically therefore closes the circle of migrations. It recalls Uncle Peter's narrative of the imaginary circle-closing in an Indian village as he is re-admitted into the community after his ambassadorial journeys (*The Swinging Bridge* 90). In the cycle of potential and real return, the physical landscape provides the space for social, metaphysical, and emotional histories to be reconfigured, reinvented, and performed. Using landscape as her narrative palimpsest, Espinet's monumentalizes Indo-Trinidadian Canadian identities. Through revisionary history, she argues for a recognition of how intra-island diasporicity, migrancy, and subsequent translocation in Canada define the Indo-Trinidadian Canadian concept of home. In repurchasing Papa's land, Kello ensures that Trinidad continues to be remembered as the point of departure and return for his family. By extension, Indo-Trinidadian Canadian literature cannot be read without an engagement with the author's multiple roots and routes across multiple landscapes. Espinet has shown that memories about the landscapes of origin are never too distant to be recalled. Kello begs Mona, " . . . you always researching Trini ting, you're the best one to go. Do this for me, Mon. I want this land, Pappy's land" (*The Swinging Bridge* 53). Canada provides Kello and Mona the wherewithal to reclaim their ancestral landscape without abandoning their Canadian one.

CECIL FOSTER

Cecil Foster's *Sleep on, Beloved*: Reflections on Afro-Caribbean Immigrant Existence in Toronto

H Nigel Thomas

Without overtly stating his purpose, Cecil Foster—ex-Barbadian journalist, novelist, cultural critic, and now professor—who immigrated to Canada in 1979 at age 28, has devoted two of his books: *Sleep on, Beloved* (1995) and *A Place Called Heaven: The Meaning of Being Black in Canada* (1996), to exploring why Canada's Blacks feel shut out of Canada's much heralded multiculturalism. A third book, *Where Race Does Not Matter: The New Spirit of Modernity* (2005), documents, among its other functions, Canada's racist heritage, for which multiculturalism is still largely an unsuccessful corrective. In the works of Foster that I focus on here—the novel *Sleep on, Beloved* and *A Place Called Heaven: The Meaning of Being Black in Canada*—one might see Toronto as metonym, a microcosm of sorts, for the rest of Canada. If we add Foster's memoir *Island Wings* (1998) to these works, the metonym extends to Britain and to the United States, the countries to which Caribbean Blacks have immigrated in large numbers.

Sleep on, Beloved depicts the destruction of a Black Toronto family and the resulting pathology on the members of that family. How Blacks resist such destruction is Foster's central preoccupation in the essays comprising *A Place Called Heaven*. My essay focuses on the pathology and alienation of Blacks in Cecil Foster's fictional Toronto. I complement my analysis of *Sleep on, Beloved* with information from *A Place Called Heaven* and use the latter to provide a context for the former. The exigencies of form—the novel and the essay—notwithstanding, I do not feel that this approach distorts Foster's intentions inasmuch as he states that the single most important goal of his writing is to faithfully record and interpret reality to the best of his ability (*Why We Write* 103). It is worth noting too that in *A Place Called Heaven* Foster's sense of life, which forms the psycho-epistemological foundation for his works, is expressed in minute detail. Underlying my analysis is the notion that place, unless the artist is inept, is always a major trope.

I begin with Foster's analysis of why institutions like the African-Canadian Heritage Foundation exist in Toronto. In his essay "What the Present Has Brought Us" (which is the first chapter of *A Place Called Heaven* as well as a de facto summary of the various issues Foster explores in that novel), Foster is attending the season's final meeting of the African-Canadian Heritage Foundation, a group of parents who gather every Saturday in a Toronto School Hall to prepare their offspring for life in what many of them consider an alien culture. These parents are actually running a complementary school program, taking the responsibility to fill in the blanks about African people in the official school curriculum. On this day, the parents want to show how far their children have come toward achieving this goal of self-education . . . This is a seminal part of the responsibility of being black in Canada: to rely on no one, not even the school system that collects your taxes or even the federal government, which preaches unity through diversity (17).

This dual education—the standard classroom instruction, developed by Euro-Canadians to provide basic educational skills and transmit a Euro-Canadian heritage, and the African-Canadian Heritage School, meeting on Saturdays, to instruct Black students about their heritage—is also present in *Sleep on, Beloved*. The fact that Suzanne performs well at the African-Canadian Heritage School but fails miserably—indeed is programmed to fail—in the Euro-Canadian school system implies that irrelevant school curricula and indifferent and hostile teachers contribute to turning Caribbean immigrant children into social misfits.

In addition to compensating for the ontological void that Black students experience in their study of the Ontario school curriculum, the African-Canadian Heritage School hopes to imbue them with the self-confidence required to negotiate "the double burden of being black, the meaning of a lifetime of discrimination"; of being always offered menial jobs; "of feeling judged by different and harsher standards at school, work and on the streets; . . . feeling spied upon and policed differently; . . . seeing virtually no reflection of [themselves] in the mainstream media and popular culture; having to deal with" expectations on the part of Whites "that to be Black means [destined] for failure or prison"; and of knowing that they will be dismissed as whiners "for speaking out against conditions that create these fears and expectations . . . " (30) This catalogue is instructive inasmuch as it replicates the problems of the Morgan family in *Sleep on, Beloved,* which will be examined below.

Two national anthems are sung at the Saturday meeting because Blacks "feel that the national anthem of the country in which [they] live does not represent [them]" (16). It is on the Black Anthem that Foster focuses, arguing that, insofar as the words reflect the dreams and aspirations of Blacks from Africa and the Diaspora, it symbolizes the fusion of Black people from continental Africa and the African Diaspora into a community united by its exclusion from mainstream Canadian society. This need for dual anthems encodes an African Canadian duality, a double consciousness much like W E B Dubois articulated it at the beginning of the twentieth century (215). And so, as far as African Canadians are concerned (Toronto is their capital), the colour line is a pivotal preoccupation in the twenty-first century. It is a colour line behind which the dominant culture mythologizes and scapegoats Canadian Blacks as "refugees, recently arrived immigrants, a drain on society, criminals and welfare bums who should be sent back to where they came from" (29).

Before I examine *Sleep on, Beloved*, it is worthwhile to look at Foster's statement about community in "What the Present Has Brought Us," inasmuch as an absence of community, as community is understood in the Caribbean, deprives Ona and Suzanne of an institution they might have employed to challenge the society and to reinforce their self worth. While many Blacks, myself included, will argue that there is no such body of people called a Canadian Black community, nor for that matter any possibility of creating one, Foster, after methodically documenting the diverse origins and interests of African Canadians, argues the reverse. Based in part on the diverse origins of those present at the

African-Canadian Heritage Association ceremony—they are from continental Africa, the various Caribbean islands, and the United States—he contends that a community of Black Canadians has been fashioned on the basis of their rejection by the White dominant society and, consequently, that Blacks are linked into a community by the common experience of oppression.

Foster argues too that the racism practised against Blacks in Canada derives from Canada's role in the colonial process, and he gives as an example the dehumanizing mythology Euro-Canadians invented to dispossess First Nations of their territory and culture. (He undertakes an expanded expatiation of this concept in *Where Race Does not Matter* (2005).) Blacks from the Caribbean and Africa, he opines, initially accept to be treated as the colonized (i.e., as providers of menial labour) when they first arrive in Canada; moreover, they make this choice, in part, because they come from countries that have been colonies. Foster further nuances this argument. He writes:

> No matter how [Blacks] strut their perceived differences, most Canadians see [them] as forming one homogenous group. And how [Blacks] are seen and treated by Canadians at large might, in the end, be the deciding factor. For how [they] are perceived will govern how [they] react to the wider community, determine whether [they] can ever become genuine Canadians, settle what conditions . . . [they] live [under] as individuals . . . friends and family. In other words, this answer implies how [Blacks] are to survive collectively as a community . . . and [their] place . . . and role[s] in Canada. (21)

Four pages later Foster more blatantly states his position. "We are all *blacked out* into a common community. And if the dominant culture agrees that the black community—a people that sold itself into colonialism—is a community, then a community we become. That is how we are forced to relate to the wider society, as a community, even if members are from different backgrounds and circumstances" (Foster's italics) (25).

There is no doubt that the Western world has problematized Africanness. From the moment Whites decided that Blacks should be enslaved because of their racial characteristics, definition by the "Other" became a fact of life for Blacks—albeit one to resisted. To the extent that the functioning of capitalist economies requires groups of exploited workers (menial labour), and to the extent that the Occident has designated Blacks thus, such a classification fits the needs of the oppressing group. And attached to this are all the coercive measures that the superstructure employs to exploit the base. But even if Foster shows the foregoing to be the case in *Sleep on, Beloved*, and even if this reader knows people whose material survival forces them to cooperate with racists, even to the point sometimes of accepting racist doctrines (many Black fundamentalist Christians, for example, believe that Blacks are the descendants the biblical Ham and are therefore divinely cursed)—this reader cannot help feeling that this is too facile an argument. The Blacks Foster is discoursing about are predominantly of Afro-Caribbean origin. There too the trickster tradition has been institutionalized, and visible cooperation coupled with invisible subversion is one of its functioning modes. Moreover, the argument can be made that the very existence of the African-Canadian Heritage Association is a frontal challenge to the attempts by the dominant culture to define Blacks. But it is also true that these West Indian "rabbits" are not conversant with the Canadian "briar patch," and consequently how to manoeuvre successfully within it, never mind manipulating it.

Let us turn now to *Sleep on, Beloved.* As I have already implied, the novel's theme is that Blacks do not find in Canada the nurture they need for self-realization. Rather they encounter a daily assault on their self-esteem. This, it should be said, is what happened to Foster's own parents who were immigrants to Great Britain. Foster's memoir *Island Wings* (1998) is a forceful account of what happened to his parents and the children they left behind. A sub-theme in *Sleep on, Beloved*, and one that is central to this essay, is that immigration is a gamble insofar as immigrants abandon the icons and symbols that integrate their psyche and encode their sense of self and being for an alien environment where they hope to attain a sense of fulfillment that eludes them in their native countries. That Foster recognizes this to be a manifestation of the Promised Land myth that infects us all is evident in *A Place Called Heaven* if only because the essays that comprise it document and analyze the various ways by which Toronto's Blacks try to keep a step ahead of psychological and cultural death in the urban wilderness of hopelessness and contempt that the dream has brought them to. The very title, *Sleep on, Beloved,* enshrouds the narrative with death. It is the title of a funeral hymn.

In some respects the plot of *Sleep on, Beloved* is not unlike the plot of novels that depict the fraudulent basis on which immigration is sometimes founded, Upton Sinclair's *The Jungle* (1906) being the most exemplary of this genre. In *The Jungle*, as in *Sleep on, Beloved*, it is the need for cheap labour, so that capitalists might be further enriched, that dictates immigration policy. In *The Invention of Canada: Literary Text and the Immigrant Imaginary*, Arnold Harrichand Itwaru analyzes ten of the "fifteen immigrant novelists who wrote and were published in English" (28) between 1947 and 1979; and of those he analyzes only one, Austin Clarke, who is non-White. Moreover, if Itwaru's criteria had not been severely winnowed to exclude novelists from the US and novels in languages other than English, not to mention works written post-1979 (27-29), the works might have numbered well over a hundred.[1]

The process of artistic distillation and the exigencies of fiction oblige Foster to reduce Canada to Toronto, and its African Caribbean population to the Morgan family and the few Blacks they interact with. Initially, in the Toronto setting, it does not matter that Ona and Suzanne—the female protagonists of *Sleep on, Beloved*—are linked to the Maroons; are the descendants of people who have resisted the attempts by colonizers to define them; follow, while in Jamaica, religious practices that reify that resistance; and know their history and are ballasted by it.

The narrative of *Sleep on, Beloved* implies that there is an invisible apparatus by which Canada cheapens its Black population. Part of this apparatus has been Canada's attitude towards its non-White immigrants.[2] Foster turns the indentureship of domestic servants from the English-speaking Caribbean into a trope that embodies colonial attitudes which, in spite of laws affirming a colour-blind immigration policy and objective selection criteria, are always present when Canada is dealing with Black immigrants. Whereas Europeans immigrated with few handicaps to Canada, pigmentation being often their only qualification—and setting aside brief periods linked to the world wars in which non-white immigration from the Caribbean was allowed—Caribbean Blacks first began to arrive in the late 1950s as domestic servants. They came, in other words, to provide menial labour for a society whose practices and ideology had already restricted its Black population to performing menial jobs. (At the thematic level Foster's character Mrs King exists primarily to instruct his readers about the pre-1960s conditions in which Blacks lived.) Moreover, the Jenkins family, to which Ona is assigned, employs her so that Mary Jenkins might go about her life as a high-fashion designer travelling around the world, or work out at the gym, or lavishly entertain when she isn't travelling; it also allows her husband to pursue his legal practice without having to worry about childcare and household chores so that he can enhance his reputation. As Mary Jenkins tells Ona, in Canada reputation, i.e., perception, is what matters. Inasmuch as the perception of Blacks as cheap menial labour undergirds the Canadian immigration policy that allows Ona to work in Canada, and to the extent that Mary and Kevin Jenkins demonstrate that they hold cheaply the value of Ona's labour and, in Kevin's case, her body, Mary's statement is a chilling one. In essence, Ona's role in the Jenkins' household is that of a slave, established on the model that Plato argues for in his Republic, the same model that Antebellum Whites of the American South instituted. It is not accidental that Foster's narrator frequently alludes to slavery at those points in the narrative where the events overtaking Suzanne and Ona are physically and psychologically brutal.

The very reason for Ona's choosing to emigrate via the "domestic scheme" is defined by the process of colonization. Ona applies to immigrate because she wants to make something of herself. She had been told by a teacher who had studied abroad that "self-fulfillment had to come from overseas. They had to accept the education offered so that when they immigrated they could fit easily into their adopted land." (57)[3] She had noted too that studying or living abroad confers the freedom to behave differently without censure. She had come to believe that immigration might redeem her from the fall in social stature that had ensued after she conceived Suzanne out of wedlock at sixteen for a man who was already married. We are to understand that the raison d'être of colonialism—in Jamaica's case, creating wealth for Britain by providing cheap resources and cheap labour and consuming expensive products manufactured in Britain—had operated to deprive Ona of opportunities for self-realization in Jamaica. Indeed, although Jamaica is by then an independent country, the legacy of colonialism had left it undeveloped. When Foster tells us in *A Place Called Heaven* that many Black immigrants to Canada enter into a colonial relationship with Canada, he is referring to examples like Ona's. It is no secret that many of the young women who came to Canada on the domestic scheme would have despised such employment in their home countries. Employed as a junior clerk with Barclays Bank at the time she leaves Jamaica, Ona, would have considered such work beneath her in Jamaica.

Moreover, married women and mothers were ineligible for the domestic indenture scheme, the reason being that Canada did not want this scheme to result in a significant increase in its non-white population. But emigrating is so important to Ona and to the other women waiting to be selected that they conceal the fact that they are mothers. Such a decision, fraught with moral consequences—if we accept that denying the existence of one's children is tantamount to denying oneself—is also an index of how desperately the women wish to immigrate. Ona's concealment of Suzanne's existence when she is interviewed in Kingston will have far-reaching consequences for both of them years later; indeed this fact is pivotal to the novel's plot. The ultimate cause of such problems, the narrative therefore suggests, is Canada's attempt to severely restrict the number of Black immigrants, in essence Canada's racist immigration policy that is rooted in colonial myths and attitudes.

The contract on which Ona comes to Canada obliges her to work for three years, after which she becomes eligible for landed immigrant[4] status. It is totally biased in her employers' favour. Breaking the contract for any reason means deportation. While the indentureship lasts, she must report to the immigration authorities, an exercise with its own built-in humiliation, since the indentured women must queue up for several hours merely to get their names on an appointment list. Built into the contract, then, is the need for non-Whites to be under tutelage, a salient feature of colonial belief and policy still evident today in Canada's policies and attitudes to its Aboriginal peoples.

To the extent that the contract imposes conditions for Immigration Canada to keep the indentured workers under surveillance but provides no monitoring system for the employers, it leaves the indentured workers, much like indentured workers in times past, subject to the employers' exploitative whims. Light work, Ona discovers, is interpreted to mean running the household and looking after the children, doing the grocery shopping, and being on call twenty-four hours per day seven days per week. The provision for two days off per week is ignored, as is annual vacation. And a gross salary of six hundred dollars per month yields a net salary of $65 after the Jenkins have charged her for room and board. When Kevin Jenkins turns to raping Ona repeatedly, he has moved from seeing her as household help to a slave he owns on pre-abolition terms. Were Ona to report such abuse to the Canadian authorities she would have been deported; and given the expectations with which she left Jamaica, and the expectations Jamaicans have of emigrant Jamaicans, Ona is trapped. When Jenkins attempts to rape her after he has forced her to have an abortion, she flees the household and automatically becomes an illegal immigrant. Had Ona been allowed to immigrate like European immigrants and to negotiate her terms of employment, such abuse would have been avoided. That the Canadian government never thought it necessary to put in place provisions to protect the indentured workers from abuse shows that it was not concerned about the workers' welfare. The threat of deportation, of which employer and employee are always aware, facilitates exploitation and renders the victim helpless. Undoubtedly, one can argue that it was because they were conditioned to attach little importance to Black humanity, to discount it even, that the White Canadians who originated this scheme saw no need for a grievance mechanism. They anticipated problems from the indentured domestic workers and stipulated the penalty of deportation for such, but saw no need to envisage problems from employers who were members of the dominant group. This is blatant racism.

What does Toronto mean for Ona at this juncture? The dream that propelled her to want to come to Canada has by now turned to a nightmare. Canada is transformed into a country where the powerful exploit the powerless, who have few rights. Her flight from Jenkins on the night that she resists his sexual predation—wandering through the maze of Toronto's unfamiliar streets for three hours in soaking raining, riding on a bus until the driver asks her to get off, without relatives or friends to call upon—epitomizes the abject, powerless situations such women found themselves in. Her plight is analogous to that of the fugitive slaves of the nineteenth century.

Ona's slippage in her legal status subserves Foster's wish to show the plight of undocumented immigrants in Toronto. Her plight and Joe Morgan's, the man she eventually marries so he could return to Canada and help her to bring her daughter to Canada, comprise the plot elements Foster uses to expose how illegal immigrants live and are treated.[5] He takes the reader through the entire process of living and working as an undocumented alien all the way to being on the plane back. Here and there the illegal immigrants may find a good friend but what they mostly find are unscrupulous employers, represented in the novel by Harold Tiltman, who dangle the hope of sponsoring them while they work them from dawn to almost midnight for less than minimum wage, and who, after exploiting them to the full, invite the immigration authorities in to arrest and deport them. For such people Toronto becomes little more than a prison, and each day is one long paroxysm of anxiety as they wonder when the immigration police will arrive. Even so, to return to Jamaica would be seen as disgrace, and Ona misleads her mother about her real situation, going so far as to promise to return soon for Suzanne.

It is worth pointing out here that in Ona's character Foster concentrates the problems indentured domestic workers and illegal immigrants face. Makeda Silvera's *Silenced: Talks with Working-Class West Indian Women about Their Lives and Struggles as Domestic Workers in Canada* (1983) contains the testimonies of ten domestic workers—and presents in documentary form what Foster explores via fiction. It should be noted too that the plight of the illegal immigrant is one of the themes in Dionne Brand's novel *Any Place, Not Here* (1996). Moreover, it wasn't necessary for Brand or Foster to read *Silenced* to be informed about the plight of illegal immigrants; their stories are a large part of the stories of Black Canadian reality.

Even for those Blacks who have landed immigrant status or are citizens, Canada is figured as a trap. Nowhere else does Foster make this clearer than in the relationships between parents and children. One of Ona's dreams when she leaves Jamaica is that in Canada she will finally be able to have her daughter Suzanne with her. Here Foster repeats the frequent refrain among Caribbean immigrants: they immigrate for their children's welfare. But Foster's narrative goes on to show that a vital component of their children's welfare, their formal education, is a process that such parents cannot control. In essence, his narrative disputes the notion that children are the beneficiaries of immigration. At one point we eavesdrop on Suzanne's thoughts as she tries to come to terms with her mother's refusal to get her out of a Buffalo prison: "Her mother was so typical of all those West Indian parents." Her thoughts go back to a night years earlier when she was standing around with a group of her friends very late in the night, none of them wanting to go home. One of them said, "Can anybody think of one youth born in the West Indies that is happy right now? I'm thinking of, say, a youth who was raised back home and come up here when he or she was almost a teenager. Any of them happy?" (29) But neither are the parents, a fact that Suzanne knows but in her youthful egocentrism avoids. Suzanne's thoughts continue and are worth quoting inasmuch as they are Foster's veiled attempt to educate his White readers—his Black readers already know the story—about the complex problems that result when parents who emigrated without their children become reunited with them.

> Even as she sat in jail . . . Suzanne reflected she still couldn't point to one happy buddy, and this was years after the question was asked. None of them got along with their parents. Particularly those who had been left behind in the Caribbean to be raised by family and friends. The story seldom varied. When they arrived in Canada they found themselves dealing with strangers, particularly fathers and stepfathers, some of whom they had never heard of until they joined them in Canada.
>
> . . . Because of this she believed she and all the immigrant children like her were a lost generation, drifting aimlessly without ties or a sense of belonging. At least this was one thing on which she and Ona agreed. How could they not agree when Ona was among the first to point out how the school system had been so good at making immigrant children feel out of place. But the schools were not the only problem, the parents were too. And that was where she and Ona disagreed. Just about everyone one of her buddies complained about the same thing: how they felt unaccepted by their parents . . .

> Many of the West Indian immigrants her age were long-term inmates of the jails. Several carried the scars from shootouts with drug dealers, others gangs or the police. Despite her faults, Suzanne knew she had done well to get as far as she had. Staying alive this long was her achievement . . . (30)

But Suzanne cannot appreciate the flaws in the immigration system that bring children and parents to this impasse. This is information available to the reader via Foster's omniscient narrator. Moreover, this unbridgeable gulf of misunderstanding is central to the novel's meaning.

This brings us back to Foster's figuration of immigration as a gamble. It is because Ona had not declared Suzanne as a dependent that she is obliged to adopt her (but declaring her, as has already pointed, would have vetoed her chances of coming to Canada). She had gambled that upon attaining landed immigrant status in Canada she would be able to remedy the lie, but she had lost. And now to get Suzanne to Canada Ona must have a husband. It is her chief reason for marrying Joe Morgan, who in turn marries her merely because he wants to be in Canada. As she reflects on her intention to marry Joe, gambling is the metaphor she seizes on to give concreteness to her intentions:

> Mentally, and to a lesser extent physically, she was tired . . . burnt-out from not having anyone to share the winnings with or to console her in the losses. If she lost again then she could go away knowing that at least she had had the guts to give it a try . . . At least she was making a stab at getting her daughter back. . . . Ah just the thought was sweet. She was going to earn her mother's smile and again hold her daughter." (116-17)

Ona will lose her gamble in ways that even she herself could not then imagine. When Suzanne arrives at age thirteen, it is to a mother she doesn't know and an adopted father she has never seen; she weaves her mother into the hostile environment she soon finds Toronto to be. Moreover, the first aspect of Toronto that impresses itself on her is her alienation from everything within it, to the point where her life during the day when her parents are absent suggests solitary confinement: "For most of the day Suzanne sat at the window and stared out." (142).

Years later she would conclude that "her mother, her stepfather, her teachers, everyone in Toronto . . . made her doubt everything she had been taught . . . Stripped her of things so innate and integral to her very being" (12)—and this to the point where she wishes to return to Jamaica. Eventually, when her adopted father begins to molest her sexually, she bifurcates into dual selves: one self remains faithful to the teachings of her grandmother and the Pocomania religion, the other accommodates without remorse her adopted father's abuse and her criminal delinquent behaviour and strip club dancing. Foster probably intends his readers to interpret this as a strategy her psyche adopts to isolate the conflicting halves of her personality in order to ensure that a part of herself remains faithful to the teachings of Grandma Nedd. But even so both selves are hostile to her mother.

This brings us to the altering power of the society, what Foster calls, as I have explained above, the society's ability to impose its definition on Blacks. After Ona's immigration problems are resolved and she finds work at a credit union, she convinces herself that she must discard the religious values she brought from Jamaica in order to become a successful Canadian. They were values that sustained her while she was in flight, while she barely survived as an illegal immigrant. The passage is worth quoting:

> In these dark days, Ona's only sustenance was to recall the stories from her mother, the tales of how they had escaped, it was the mere dream of freedom, someday a great and total emancipation coming, that stopped their foreparents' willing return to captivity, to the cotton and cane fields or to cleaning, cooking and caring for the children in the exploiters' homes. (87)

In Ona's abandonment of these beliefs the narrative sets up a contrast between her own and Suzanne's method of negotiating Toronto reality. I will discuss this later.

Ona even accepts the stereotype that the descendants of the earliest Blacks to settle in Canada are shiftless and obsequious in order to fit better into the roles white society forces Blacks into. It suggests an eagerness on Ona's part to mutilate her psyche in exchange for some nebulous reward she vaguely terms "getting ahead." But her alteration, as I have already shown, begins long before then—and against her will—even as she is planning to emigrate, with her preparedness to deny Suzanne's existence, and later in the abortion she submits to (which in Pocomania doctrine means damning her soul)[6] so that she might remain in Canada. By the time Suzanne arrives, Ona's frustrations with racial prejudice are overwhelming; the rant of an embittered woman who feels cheated on every hand and by everyone is what Joe and Suzanne are forced to listen to each evening. She is a woman bereft of the psychological structures necessary to neutralize the daily hatred she encounters. She has become an empty shell of a human being.

I have stated earlier that the attitudes that Blacks come up against seem to sketch a predetermined pattern for the way the dominant society treats Blacks. In Ona's case, it means watching the promotions she seeks go to the White young women she has trained, ostensibly because there is an unwritten code in the society that better paying jobs should go to Whites; in Suzanne's case, this means that in the fierce competition by students for their teachers' attention Blacks are ignored. The blatant message in this practice is that in Canadian society the needs of Whites take priority over those of non-Whites. Never being called upon to answer the teachers' questions, and having their accents mocked when they do, Suzanne and her Black friend Bobby Ali disrupt their classes to protest the belittlement they are subjected to, and come to value their disruptions over compliance with White bigotry. In his conversation with Ona, the principal shows how inflexible the education system is, and demonstrates that Blacks will either fit into the system or get pushed to the margins, which is what happens to Suzanne in spite of her mother's protests and court challenges to prevent it. His motto might well be: adapt or perish. It is the society's way to punish those who do not conform, and conformity means wordlessly accepting the humiliation the system subjects Blacks to. Eventually Suzanne and Bobby Ali would resort to theft to vent their anger on a society that has rejected and cheapened them.

Three details of the novel are worth focusing on: Suzanne's recurring nightmare, Joe's theft, and Ona's eventual madness. The first and the last are interrelated. Not a small source of the friction between Ona and

Suzanne is the fact that Ona has abandoned her religion and is pushing Suzanne to do likewise. Suzanne is repelled by the fact that Ona had led Grandma Nedd to believe that she was faithfully practising the Pocomania rituals and was still being succoured by them.

Suzanne's nightmare—which occurs "at least once a month . . . ten years after her arrival in Canada, after she had gone through the Children's Aid Society's foster homes, and six years after she started to live on her own" (12-13), and especially at moments when she is facing a moral crisis—is a series of dream symbols that oppose her sense of self against the forces that assail her. This nightmare, more than any other of Foster's devices, presents coming to Canada as a monstrous act of betrayal by her grandmother and those who let her leave Jamaica, for it is in the induction into sexual degradation that the nightmare is figured. It always begins with the farewell service Suzanne attended before coming to Canada. The drums, which in the Pocomania rituals symbolize Black resistance to slavery and which Suzanne links to the Rastafarian edict against immigration, remind her of promises she made to stay firmly grounded in her religious teachings. But it is the transmogrification of Ona that most effectively portrays how Suzanne comes to regard her mother, who represents what Suzanne does not want to become—a traitor to the history and beliefs of her people:

> Inside the plane, naked and dancing, was Suzanne's mother. Her face had been painted with so much makeup it became a demonic mask, just like one of the trickster goddesses Grandma Nedd always warned Suzanne against. It was nothing . . . nothing like the mask Mira Nedd wore when she became more than just Suzanne's grandmother. Inside the mask, Mira was transformed into the spiritual power that was represented in all women, all mothers, in all things fertile, in the air, in the water and on land. When Grandma Nedd said she was just like Mother Earth. (14)

But regarding her mother:

> Every time the light changed the features of this woman that was Suzanne's mother altered. At times a smiling woman; other times cackling, demeaning and ugly, the hands flying every which way . . . All the time her mother danced, pulled at her

> breasts, at her public hair, swung her legs like a young woman dancing naked under the lights." (15)

At this point the doors of the plane close and end all possibility of Suzanne's escaping. "When her mother reached out to touch her with talon-like hands, like an eagle swooping down on its prey, Suzanne screamed and jumped up from the dream." (15)

That the dream itself represents the split in Suzanne's personality is evident. But paradoxically it will, following Mira Nedd's death and Ona's collapse into insanity, serve as a catalyst to heal the split in Suzanne's psyche.

I have already mentioned that it is as a gamble that Ona characterizes her marriage to Joe Morgan. Foster subsumes into the gambling metaphor Joe's actual gambling. This is meant to suggest more than a life adrift. It can be argued that both Joe and Ona are participants in a gambling game. Until Joe gains landed immigrant status, Ona holds the trump cards, but once he has done so, they are in his hands. Joe's gambling nature is evident in all that he does—his seduction of Suzanne, his taking a woman into Ona's bed, and finally his defrauding the Toronto Transit Commission to feed his gambling habit. But Joe's desire to remain in Canada is itself fuelled by the promised-land dream, and he gambles that entering into a marriage he does not want will make it possible. But—and we are forced to take this upon Ona's word—Canadian society, which holds other trump cards, has already determined Joe's place, and it is to be in a Toronto Transit Commission cage. When this fact is taken into consideration, literal gambling, which leads to his theft of TTC money, is a desperate distraction by a man whose life has lost any sense of purpose, a man who has long lost whatever morality and dreams he brought from Barbados.

From the beginning, Foster's narrator, in preparing us for Ona's insanity, shows us that Ona gambles with stakes too intricate for her to measure, beginning with her decision to conceal her motherhood in order to immigrate to Canada, and always with the other holding the trump card. The highest stake is the one she is least aware of: her exchange of her Jamaican sense of self for some vague promise of success. When on Christmas Eve day she dons the attire of the Pocomanians and "journeys" in Eaton Centre, we know that the highest stake of all is her sanity. If we examine this in light of Ona's coming to Canada ostensibly to redeem herself, we see in her insanity a bitter irony, especially if we accept the Judaeo-Christian belief that redemption requires sacrifice. All along she has been the sacrifice—has been sacrificed by her employers, by the institutions that confer such power on her employers, by Joe, and even by Suzanne. By the time Suzanne arrives, Ona is a shell of woman with a very brittle psyche. Perhaps the catalyst for her final demise is her return to Jamaica to bury Mira Nedd according to the rites of the Pocomania religion. It plunges her into seeing what her sojourn has been since she left Jamaica, and into assessing what she had thrown away ostensibly to lighten her burdens. Few can psychically dismember themselves the way Ona has, become aware of it, and thereafter remain sane. In insanity, she seeks to recover the identity she had sacrificed; paradoxically, to regain that earlier self, she must yield up her sanity. Put differently, immigration for Ona, unknown to her, had been a Faustian bargain in which the Devil took all, promised much, and gave nothing.

Paradoxically, and in an excruciating manifestation of the sacrificial motif, Ona's insanity is the catalyst that reintegrates Suzanne's psyche. In yet another paradox, it also saves Suzanne's life, inasmuch as that day, Christmas Eve, the distraction caused by her mother's insanity prevents her from participating in the hold-up staged by Bobby Ali's gang, in which the gang members are killed. Because of her mother's insanity Suzanne finds a mission for her life, getting custody of her toddler brother, who as a result of Ona's psychosis is in the custody of the Children's Aid Society.

It can be argued that Suzanne's clinging to the proud history her grandmother inculcated in her drove her to resist the efforts of Canadian society to reshape her for its uses. Her partial pathology, her dual self, engendered to isolate the pristine from the corrupt, enables her to function, whereas Ona, who abandons her groundings, disintegrates into full-blown madness—as a way of recovering the self she has abandoned.

Undoubtedly Foster is holding up an aspect of the Jamaican (or Caribbean or African Canadian) component of the multiculturalism Canada purports to foster to show how the racism built into Canada's figuration of itself undermines the lofty goals of racial equality and multiculturalism. The travails of the Morgan family in Toronto, Canada's most multicultural city, depict how such insidious racism works. Foster later states (2006) that

> one of the things I was trying to do in *Sleep on, Beloved* was to show the hidden costs of immigration—which in effect were not so hidden; in fact, they are quite visible . . . I wanted to look at the cost to these women [single Caribbean women on the domestic scheme]: socially, they are isolated; they are cut off from friends and relatives—the women they bond with, the women who teach them how to socialize—those women who are vital transmitters of the culture, an essential part of Caribbean reality. One of the tropes I relied on to show this disconnection is dancing as a reflection of these characters' innermost spirituality. But by the time reader gets to the third generation of this family in Toronto, by then cut off from any form of spiritual revitalization, dancing is no longer for divine reasons, not for God but for money. That spiritual link is broken and the characters are bereft and must struggle to fill the void. (Interview 106)

On the broader theme of immigration in his work, Foster was asked to comment on the following: "In your novel *No Man in the House* and in your memoir *Island Wings*, . . . emigration is fuel, shredder, and pathogen. For [your character] Howard it is initially fuel and then shredder. For you and your brothers it was similar. Perhaps pathogen is too strong a word." He replied:

> Pathogen is not too strong a word. If there's a reason to my writing, it has been to confront that pathology. Non-immigrants do not know the emotional cost of immigration. I did, from the time I was two, when the immigration process took my parents. They went elsewhere, well-intentioned, in search of a good life, and were devoured by the process . . . Going to "the Promised Land" was not life; it was death. What could be more pathological? (Interview 104)

A study of Foster's entire corpus—five novels, four scholarly works, and a memoir—would reveal his profound commitment to exploring African Diasporic ontology via fiction and non-fiction. Implicit in his novels is the notion that art could entertain and enlighten. His choice of forms, fiction and the essay, reveals that he wishes to engage the debate at all levels: the popular and the scholarly. Foster's focus on the Morgan family allows his reader to see the ramifications of racist historical decisions. In his essay *Where Race Does Not Matter: The New Spirit of Modernity,* after documenting Canada's apartheid-type historical decisions, he argues that unless correctives are undertaken, Canada's lofty goal of being a multicultural society is doomed to failure. *Sleep on, Beloved,* it could be argued, portrays significant aspects, to use a chapter title from Foster' *A Place Called Heaven,* of "what the past has brought us." But Foster, who sees his work, fiction and nonfiction, as a complementary whole, thinks that Canada can undertake the measures to prevent the ongoing psychic destruction that its past policy now wreaks on its Black citizens.

RABINDRANATH MAHARAJ

Dismantled Domestics, Loneliness, and Creative Coping in Rabindranath Maharaj's *The Amazing Absorbing Boy*

Shoilee Khan

Rabindranath Maharaj's novel *The Amazing Absorbing Boy* (2010) explores the modern immigrant experience through the perspective of seventeen-year-old Samuel, a young man emerging from the tumultuous social heat and energy of Trinidad to stand on the precipice of adulthood in the unfamiliar and seemingly fantastical city of Toronto. This familiar narrative—dislodgement from country of origin, turbulent period of transition, and a concluding period of integration into new and now known territory—is common in immigrant narratives, but is here filtered through the perspective of an adolescent whose experience is centered on the reciprocal relationship between loneliness and imagination. Maharaj's narrative then describes the emergence of a creative thinker and producer.

Studies on the significance of loneliness acknowledge that the "need to belong" drives our thoughts and motivations, shaping the way we relate to others and requiring fulfillment in the form of "frequent, positive interactions with other people" (Heinrich and Gullone 2006, 695). This need for belonging points towards a dire, primal yearning for "intimacy, warmth, a sense of worth, and frequent confirmation of . . . [our] identities" (696). It is sought through relationships, and when these relationships are dismantled or do not live up to expectations, the experience of loneliness is felt. Loneliness in adolescence is of particular significance, with a transition from parents to peers as attachment figures and the consequent beginning of self-discovery.

The fruition of complex and abstract self-perception is of particular importance when considering Samuel's development through adolescence in *The Amazing Absorbing Boy*. Sam is conceptualized as a foreigner in a foreign land, an individual grappling with intense loneliness and inadvertently using it as an avenue to creativity. Sam's loneliness pervades and arises from the physical spaces that he inhabits, both domestic and public, each space functioning as an instigator for his imaginative coping, a process that leads to eventual creative production. The negative experiences of involuntary aloneness propel Sam into compulsive and cathartic imaginative episodes where he establishes a sense of agency and independence. He creates for himself the necessary mental space to engage with imaginative worlds that allow him to process his loneliness as a positive and empowering form of engagement.

Traditionally, domestic space has been represented as a space of retreat, with interiors as female-centred spaces of orderly refuge and peace. For example, in much of Jane Austen's work, drawing rooms act as spaces of communal engagement. These spaces billow with female energy that functions as a source of nourishment for the rest of the household, and by extension, for the community at large. In other works, such as the novels of Charles Dickens, the domestic space is conflated with public space, the typical female haven of the interior disrupted by the constant intrusion of the outside world.

The private spaces that Sam inhabits are devoid of female presence and are in perpetual transition. They are spaces of dislodgement and emptiness that work to expel instead of to embrace, creating an internal state of tumult in Sam, a lack of stability and familial connection he so potently desires, thus instilling in him a deep sense of loneliness. This loneliness serves as a trigger for Sam to use fantasy-fuelled coping mechanisms that result in an entry into a unique creative process.

In Mayaro, Trinidad, the private domestic space that Sam and his mother inhabit undergoes a process of transition that begins during his mother's decline through terminal illness. Their home is never rendered as a space of quiet retreat—we begin with a home in flux from the very start, his mother's appearance changing in rapid and almost fantastical ways as she suffers through four months of illness: " . . . all her wavy hair

[was] falling out so that instead of looking prettier than all the Mayaro women, she began to resemble a caged monkey inside Lighthouse rumshop" (2). Sam's perception of his mother's decline is indicative of the rapid infiltration of something strange and foreign that inhabits his primary space of familiarity and the core representation of his home—his mother. She morphs from a spirited, pretty woman moving freely through town to an animal caged, a mockery of her former self. In the weeks that follow, Sam observes as his mother "began dressing up in fancy clothes . . . [Sam] had never seen before . . . " (2) On his return from school, he enters his home each day to witness "her in a new and unfamiliar dress. They looked expensive, with sashes, embroidered collars, and frilly hems" (2). Both images are fantastical and grotesque in their renditions and signal a disruption within the home. The centre of the home, Sam's mother, undergoes a transformation that renders her unfamiliar to her son. The objects she adorns herself with—the fancy, frilly dresses—are objects of both necessity and excess. As her body deteriorates, she uses these ostentatious coverings as a second, artificial skin, her presence replaced by costume and façade, layers of fabric filling out the vacancy her disappearing body leaves behind.

When Sam returns to his home three weeks after his mother's funeral, he finds himself navigating the unsettling landscape of a ghost house. He observes that "the curtains had been removed and there were drapes and doilies over all the pictures" (7). At this initial visit, Sam sits on a "chair facing the window and look[s] out at the road" (7) before being startled awake by a sound from the kitchen—where his mother would have been—and feeling a jolt of fear and surprise, "bolted up and ran straight down the road, not stopping until [. . . he] reached Uncle Boysie's shop" (7). The removal of the curtains from the windows indicates a transition of the private space into an undefined "threshold" where the two worlds—public and private—collide. The curtains, which separate the private space of the home from onlookers on the road are removed and placed over family photographs that adorn the home. When the curtain is removed from the window, it removes the barrier that once protected the home from the public gaze, an intrusion from the public sphere. When the curtain is then placed over the family photographs, it marks the end of the familial connection that Sam so keenly desires.

This, however, can signify both the blotting out of the private sphere and the protection of what remains. The phantom sounds from the kitchen send Sam "straight down the road" and into his Uncle's shop, a space of consumer interaction, filled with oddities that are collected, bought, and sold to the public. Sam has been expelled from his home by the imagined presence of a ghost-mother.

As Sam moves through the city after his mother's death, he inhabits the role of a transient observer:

> . . . dead mangrove crabs looked like birds that had lost their feathers and pitched to earth. The evening high tides usually washed ashore dozens of silvery fishes but their eyes shone so brightly it seemed as if they didn't want to die. Sometimes there were families from town gathered around their cars . . . They always asked the same questions: "Which school you from, sonnyboy?" and "How come you walking all by yourself?" (7)

Here, Sam's observations are indicative of his grief, the death imagery contrasting between the urgency to live and the inevitability of death. The de-feathered birdlike crabs that are "pitched to earth" alongside waves of silvery fish washing ashore, the potent desire to live shining through bright eyes, signals Sam's internal conflict, his straddling the two worlds of life and death. Sam walks alone and confronts a direct question about his aloneness—"how come you walking all by yourself?" by embracing the moniker "nowheriean" as an identifier:

> Because I'm a *nowhereian,* I thought once, and immediately the word seemed flavoured with recklessness. Like an adventurer moving from place to place with no friends or family to hook on to him. Like the Silver Surfer but no Galactus to command him . . . (7)

In this way, Sam seeks a sense of empowerment from his new, transient status as a boy who not only walks alone through his town, but must walk alone through life. He reclaims the derogatory term used to describe his father's lack of responsibility and lack of connection to his family and rebrands it as a fantastical superhero identity that affords him a sense of agency as well as an outlet for the depth of grief he feels but cannot express.

This process of dislodgement, the dismantling of the domestic sphere, and the subsequent loneliness and creative production that follows, continues with Sam's removal to his father's apartment in Toronto. The private space his father occupies in Rexdale is devoid of both familial affection and nourishment and creates in Sam a depth of loneliness that necessitates a retreat into the public sphere. Like his mother's home in Mayaro, the home Sam lands in upon arrival in Canada is in a state of disintegration. This is especially apparent when Sam, sitting across from a noncommunicative father on a bus, observes the city for the first time. Looking out the window, he sees that "people with coats were walking briskly, not chatting in groups like in Trinidad. They all looked faded, like dematerializing comic book ghosts" (18). These initial impressions of Sam's new city are devoid of colour and warmth, the isolation of passersby emphasized by pale faces and stooped postures that lack the vibrancy needed to live as the comic book heroes that Sam admires. They are ghosts moving alone through the city—a reflection of the isolation felt by Sam at the disappointing reunion he has just experienced with his father. As the bus rumbles on through the city, Sam observes his father: "In the evening light he looked pale and sad, like someone sitting in a dark, damp place like the Batcave, and knowing his schemes were slipping away one by one" (18). Sam's observations are tinged with sadness, but they also carry a depth of understanding that aids in helping him cope and even connect with his father. Sam's feeling of loneliness is intensified when he sits at the kitchen table waiting for his father to open up a conversation, offer an explanation for his absence, or at the very least, show a semblance of interest in Sam's life. Instead, Sam inhabits the role of observer and watches his father move through the kitchen, a domestic space in acute distress.

> The lower shelf was lined with old newspapers. He got out a package of some sort, sniffed it, and threw its contents into a bucket between the stove and the fridge. There were bread scraps on the tiled floor and a crumpled box of fruit juice that he kicked towards the bucket as he returned to the living room. (20)

With this air of bitter carelessness, Sam's father moves through the kitchen with little purpose, apparently unaffected by his son's presence. He does not seem to possess the ability to fulfill the basic responsibilities of a father; his ramble through the kitchen is a show of reckless disregard and serves as a portrait of a man who has succumbed to resignation. His "schemes" for the fruition of a vibrant life in Canada lie in tatters, represented by food leftovers littering the kitchen—a traditionally female space of nourishment for the body and spirit. He cannot feed Sam because he has hardly learned to feed himself. He has nothing to offer aside from the remnants of a life that he no longer dreams about.

When his father leaves the apartment and does not return for several days, Sam finds himself trapped in a warped domestic space without food or guidance:

> By midday I had a bigger concern: what if he did not return? . . . I am not ashamed to say I panicked that day. I was in a strange place. I knew no one except for my father. I had no idea about any of the rules or laws. The apartment looked smaller each hour and I began to feel like these movie actors trapped inside closing-in walls. I rushed to the balcony and watched people walking about on sidewalks and pavements. (27)

Sam's domestic space is a threat to his wellbeing, feeding a slowly growing panic. Sam is acutely aware of his isolation and aloneness. Far removed from anything knowable and familiar, devoid of the familial connection that he needs and desires, he moves into a threshold space that allows him access to a world outside his domestic environment. From the balcony he observes life and draws comfort from the awareness of other people. This triggers a memory of his mother's gaze upon photographs of herself and Sam's father as a young couple. He creates a story that serves as sustenance for his survival with his father. Describing the photograph, Sam recalls:

> Whenever I asked my mother about this couple, she always said it was two people who had disappeared. That made the picture interesting and mysterious and I sometimes made up little stories to explain their disappearance. The most interesting was they had moved to one of the misty hills in the forest, past the radar station, where they looked down on a river

> flowing into the beach and the manatees playing among the water reeds. (35)

He begins to indulge in a fantasy that reconciles his parents and places them in an environment that allows them freedom from the confines of a physical home, but also removes them from the gaze of the public eye. They become observers instead of participants and this affords Sam a sense of peace: "The next day, with this picture in my mind, I felt a tiny bit of happiness and decided I would try to understand my father's coldness" (35). Through fantasy, Sam is able to reconcile himself to the reality of his father's behavior and commit himself to action instead of passive acceptance. Thus begins Sam's journey as a creative problem-solver, he uses stories and daydreams as a method of creative coping and eventual relief.

M G VASSANJI

"The Multinational's Song": M G Vassanji's Work in Canadian Context[1]

Laura Moss

On an early version of his author website, M G Vassanji made his own multinational status clear, "If pressed, I describe myself as an IndoAfrican Canadian writer. Attempts to box me in I find abhorrent."[2] One of the vanguard of writers from the South Asian diaspora in Canada,[3] Vassanji is central to contemporary Canadian literature. Awarded the Order of Canada in recognition of his literary service to the country, he has also won the Commonwealth Writers' Prize (Africa region) and twice won the Giller Prize, among other notable honours. His fiction is widely studied in academic contexts, read in book clubs, reviewed in high-profile media venues, and bought by a Canadian audience and by global readers alike. Further, his work has been translated into Dutch, French, German, Hindi, Italian, Japanese, Latvian, Portuguese, Spanish, Turkish, and Swahili. Full of imagined engagements with migration, globalization, and flexible conceptions of home, citizenship, and national affiliation, Vassanji's fiction appeals to a wide readership. In addition to being a writer of fiction and nonfiction, the author has also spent more than thirty years as a publisher and editor with a focus on expanding Canadian literary culture to include writing from South Asian Canadian writers and from "abroad." On both sides of literary production, he has been instrumental in opening up spaces for a multiplicity of voices in Canadian literary contexts as he has worked to break narrow national categorizations by publishing narratives that engage with multiple locations, constituencies, cultures, languages, and ideas. With the recognition of his personal trajectories, Vassanji is multiply read as an African writer who immigrated to Canada and who, because of his heritage, fit into the diasporic framework of South Asian writing. Vassanji's negotiation of the complexities of "Indo," "African," and "Canadian" identities in his own history are mirrored in his fiction and nonfiction (set in India, Kenya, Tanzania, Canada, and beyond) as well as in his own editorial and critical work. Further, I suspect that Vassanji's quiet refusal to be boxed in by expectation (of nationality, religious faith, or of genre, I might add) echoes the desire of global readers to think laterally about identity and place.

Critic Simon Gikandi begins his entry for Vassanji in the *Columbia Guide to East African Literature in English since 1945* with a statement of difficulty: "The novelist M G Vassanji is hard to categorize because of his hybrid background" (172). Nearly every promotional piece and review of his work trots out international credentials: born in Kenya, educated in Tanzania and the USA where he earned a PhD in theoretical nuclear physics, Vassanji moved to Canada in 1978 to take up a postdoctoral fellowship with Atomic Energy of Canada and later to become a research associate at the University of Toronto (1980-89). With the success of his first novel, *The Gunny Sack* (1989), he left his work as a physicist and became a full-time writer settling permanently in Toronto with his family, and often visiting East Africa and later India. During this time he also co-created and co-edited the *Toronto South Asian Review* (TSAR) (published since 1993 as the *Toronto Review of Contemporary Writing Abroad*). Prolific, he has published six more novels—*No New Land* (1990), *The Book of Secrets* (1993), *Amriika* (2000); *The In-Between World of Vikram Lall* (2003), *The Assassin's Song* (2007), and *Nostalgia* (2016); two books of short stories, *Uhuru Street* (1990) and *When She Was Queen* (2005); two memoirs, *A Place Within: Rediscovering India* (2008) and *And Home was Kariakoo: A Memoir of East Africa* (2015); and a biography of the Quebec writer *Mordecai Richler* (2009) for the Penguin Extraordinary Canadians series. Much of Vassanji's fiction and nonfiction moves between North America, East Africa, and India, as he writes of the countries of his birth, his early education, and his adult years with a critical awareness of the implications of collective history on individual lives. In turn, he weaves individual stories into an often-communal narrative. The novels map a global literary landscape that includes Canada and Tanzania, Kenya and India, America and the rest of the world. Whether they go from the Nakuru valley to the snowy banks of Lake Ontario, or from university in Dar es Salaam to anti-Vietnam protests in Massachusetts, his characters often experience both a love of place and sense of alienation from that place. Fittingly, much of his writing is about home, finding home, being at home, and/or feeling homeless. Broadly, his work is concerned with opening up and rethinking history, with the vicissitudes of migration and diasporic movement, with exile and return, with home, with memory, with the pain of nostalgia, and with family and cross-generational conflict.

What is not often mentioned in scholarship on Vassanji's fiction is his role as an editor and critic. Since the 1980s he has been instrumental in helping to build a strong and recognizable South Asian Canadian writing community. When Vassanji arrived in Canada, many first-generation Canadians were vociferously arguing for the need to open up Canadian literature (and Canadian culture) to more minority voices and stories. He and three like-minded people, his wife and two classmates from school, joined forces to found the *Toronto South Asian Review* in 1981, which received support from various scholars, critics, and writers. The journal's initial mission was to "make accessible to a wide audience literature that traces some part of its inheritance and meaning in the culture, traditions and history of the Indian subcontinent" (1, qtd in Mukherjee 30). The binding trace of inheritance is key here as a means to link artists from India, Africa, and the Caribbean with those already in North America.

In 1985 TSAR expanded to become a press as well as a journal and launched its inaugural collection of essays, *A Meeting of Streams: South Asian-Canadian Literature*, edited by the editor of the *TSAR* journal and the new co-editor of the press, M G Vassanji. Critic Arun Mukherjee notes that *A Meeting of Streams* is "the first time one comes across the idea of a grouping of writers defined by their ethnicity" in English Canadian writing (24). On the blurb for *A Meeting of Streams*, Vassanji's collection itself declares a need for the "grouping together of concerted and many-sided look at the literature" of writers of South Asian diasporic origins. The critical essays highlight not only the very *existence*, which at the time was crucial to emphasize, but also the *significance* and *merit* of a range of literature from a variety of South Asian communities in Canada as they negotiate the local and historical specificities of that writing. In his introduction, Vassanji notes the broad question asked by the contributors to the collection: "What should South Asian Canadian literature, and its place in Canadian literature, be?" (5) That the answers differ, with some "concurrences and divergences" is precisely the point of the collection (5). The point that Mukherjee makes, through Vassanji, is that "the reality is that the South Asian Canadian community does not have a monolithic perspective, and nor do its writers" (38) but, Mukherjee adds, there is a tentative sense of a shared history that joins writers on the same platform. In noting the potentially essentializing implications of the term "South Asian," Mukherjee cites Vassanji's own wrestling, in 1993 shortly before the journal name-change, with the label he helped to popularize: "I have never sensed a passion behind that label 'South Asian'—no political front, not even a loosely defined conscious aesthetic or the probing for one: it seemed to be simply a very convenient and the least discomfiting umbrella to fit under" (6, qtd in Mukherjee 31). The umbrella term that Vassanji and TSAR strategically employed effectively helped to create a critical mass of readers and critics invested in the field of South Asian studies within Canada.

Over the course of the 1980s, TSAR further opened its mandate to focus on fiction, nonfiction, and poetry of "New Canadian and World Writing," considering for "publication writers of any origin whose work in some way is inspired by the diversity of our world (specifically Canada) and the interaction and sharing of cultures."[4] Two decades later, TSAR became Mawenzi House (Mawenzi being the name of the second peak of Kilimanjaro), with a continued mandate to bring "to the reading public fresh new writing from Canada and across the world that reflects the diversity of our rapidly globalizing world, particularly in Canada and the United States."[5] Acting as co-editor of the journal and the press (TSAR and Mawenzi) over the years, Vassanji has played a key role in establishing South Asian Canadian intellectual and entrepreneurial groups, and concomitantly, he has had substantial impact on the cultural and critical frameworks that have proceeded to define his own literary reception within Canada.

Still, those at TSAR were not alone in linking Vassanji's work to that of other South Asian writers in Canada. Indeed, Vassanji has been regularly included alongside Rohinton Mistry (born in India), Neil Bissoondath (born in Trinidad), and Michael Ondaatje (born in Sri Lanka), some of the most central and successful contemporary Canadian writers.[6] Conversely, as if to emphasize his Canadianness and the international appeal of his work on India, the reviews quoted for *A Place Within* and *Assassin's Song* on the Penguin India webpage are from the *Globe and Mail* and *Quill and Quire*, both published in Toronto.[7] His publishers have taken full advantage of the group affiliation as he has often been marketed alongside writers from India, Sri Lanka, and Pakistan, as well as from Africa and Canada. Such canny associational marketing comes out of both the South Asian Canadian literary community's strategic affiliation and out of publishers' recognition of group appeal in a popularized postcolonial climate.

As with his strategic grouping under the South Asian umbrella with TSAR, Vassanji's early writing explores stories that fit under the same umbrella. His first work set in Canada, *No New Land*, follows the Lalani family in Don Mills, a suburb of Toronto, as they respond to an accusation of sexual assault by the father. This quiet, and at times deeply ironic, novel is about family, alienation, religion, self-doubt, and often failed attempts at inter-generational communication. It is also Vassanji's least successful novel as it follows a somewhat formulaic engagement with "immigrant issues." Subsequent work is less overtly concerned with marking a place for the quotidian stories of East Africans in Canada. It just does it. In the 2005 collection of short stories set partially in Toronto, *When She Was Queen*, Vassanji takes on a similar set of themes as in *No New Land* but this time is more nuanced in his execution. While the majority of Vassanji's fiction travels between North America, East Africa, and India, his work persists in drawing on thematic concerns that appeal in Canada: liminality, negotiating multiple-identities, multiculturalism, immigration, citizenship, and historicity among them.[8]

As the 1990s progressed, the prevailing critical trend in Canadian criticism shifted from reading the novels of new Canadians set outside Canada as mainly supplemental to national imperatives to recognizing them as central to and in Canadian literature. Publications and publishing houses like TSAR helped instigate change to reflect the significant transformations in the larger Canadian society. The shift in attitudes to literary works parallels the reconfiguration of demographics in Canada and alterations in attitudes about Canadian constitutive identities over the past forty years. According to Statistics Canada, on the 2011 Canadian Census, people reported close to 200 places of birth and, between 2006 and 2011, 56.9 percent of newcomers to Canada hailed from Asia (StatsCan's categorization), including South Asia. In contrast, in 1971, when the first multiculturalism policy was introduced in parliament, Asians accounted for 12 percent of newcomers.[9] In cultural terms, Vassanji's increased visibility and popularization, signalled by the winning of national and international acclaim, is often cited as exemplary in illustrating the dismantling of separate categories such as "multicultural" or "ethnic" to a reconfigured "mainstream" Canadian literature. However, this was not always the case. When *The Book of Secrets* was first awarded the Giller Prize and when Rohinton Mistry's *A Fine Balance* won the same award the following year (1995), there were grumblings in the national media about whether novels that were set in Africa and India should be considered eligible for an award honouring the best of *Canadian* writing. Now, over two decades later, when much of the finest, and most financially successful and globally well-received, fiction written by Canadians tells stories about elsewhere and is written by first-generation Canadians, such a criticism could no longer even find its feet or, hopefully, be given press.

Vassanji has often exhibited concern about the relationship between his own writing and the expectations of Canadian audiences. In his 2006 editorial for the journal *Canadian Literature* titled "Am I a Canadian Writer?" Vassanji asks a question of himself as a way of answering other second person self-interrogations: "Whom do you write for? Who is your audience?" (7) In response, Vassanji has voiced his desire to move beyond what he sees as the expectations of "Canadianness," arguing that "We all know the Prairie-grandmother novel; the growing-up-in-Newfoundland-or-Nova-Scotia, walking-along-the-beach-with-an-ancestor novel; the World War I novel; the cool-thirtysomething or –fortysomething Vancouverite novel" (8). His method, echoing the trend with most contemporary Canadian authors, is to write novels without resorting to these well-worn types or geographically-determined genres. Instead, he suggests remapping Canadian literary landscapes to include Kenya and Cambodia, India, and Rwanda: "the idea I am putting forward is that new Canadians bring their stories with them, and these stories then become Canadian stories" (12). For Vassanji, Canadian stories are malleable enough to encounter the mass migrations of people from around the world. They also withstand explorations of personal history and cultural memory in the countries of origin of their writers.

It is useful to note that Vassanji is far from alone in approaching the nation in such open terms. The difference in the contemporary framework is that writing about people and places outside Canada is no longer viewed as an adjunct to central Canadian writing. Now, Madeleine Thien's *Do Not Say We Have Nothing*, David Chariandy's *Soucouyant*, Anita Rau Badami's *Can You Hear the Nightbird Call*, and Dionne Brand's *What We All Long For* join Vassanji's *The In-Between World of Vikram Lall*, for instance, as prominent examples of Canadian novels that span histories, generations, and countries and tell Canadian stories—in Canada and China, Trinidad, India, and Kenya.

Vassanji's rise to literary stardom coincides with an international post-Rushdie hunger for historical revisionist writing in postcolonial contexts. The cover of *The Gunny Sack* makes this link explicit calling it "Africa's answer to *Midnight's Children*." While he does not *chutnify* history in the novel, Vassanji does reinscribe East African history to showcase a multigeneration genealogical Indian presence.[10] As such he engages in the act of rewriting history to include the stories of those not previously included in national epics. In his first novel, as well as in *A Book of Secrets* and *The In-Between World of Vikram Lall*, Vassanji carefully ties together several generations of Indian family stories in East Africa through material objects (a gunny sack, a colonial diary, books, and money), reminiscences of mercantile methodologies, and displaced cultural memories. He narrates the impact of colonialism on African subjects and Indian merchants and labourers as he follows the presence and afterlife of British and German imperialism. Glossing his own motivation to write *The In-Between World of Vikram Lall*, Vassanji explains that the novel is intended to address a gap in knowledge: "Books set in Kenya, especially those made into movies or TV serials for Masterpiece Theatre, glorifying the English aristocracy in Kenya, hardly mention the presence of Indians, who played an important role in the growth of Nairobi, the building of the railway, and the politics of the country. Their dilemma was that they were neither white nor black; and they were both Asian and African" (author website). Such an intention to narrate, and thereby complicate, the histories of Indians in Africa is carried through several of his novels. As Gikandi notes, Vassanji's fiction is consistent in its exploration of the themes he began to explore in *The Gunny Sack*, particularly "the struggle by Indians in Africa, and later North America, to come to terms with their multiple histories of displacement while rebuilding their communities in exile" (173).

In *The In-Between World of Vikram Lall*, for instance, Vassanji traces the individual legacy of the struggle for independence in Kenya, particularly the Mau Mau uprising, initially through the eyes of small children and then as they grow into a world of love, violence, corruption, and greed. Vassanji does not shy away from showing the pain of the independence movement. One of the early pivotal events in the novel is the brutal murder of Vikram's childhood friends who are British. To balance this, however, we see innocent Kikuyu men targeted, arrested, and tortured because of who they are and not because of what they have done. The titular character often refers to himself as apolitical but he cannot help but be caught up in the politics of independence and national growth. As an "Asian" in colonial Kenya, he often finds himself and his family in between the British and the Kikuyu, in particular. The story of Vikram's coming of age parallels in time the story of Kenya and shows how quickly perspectives can change. Indeed, for example, over the course of the novel, the Mau Mau are first perceived as terrorists and then, after Independence, they are celebrated as freedom fighters, only to be depicted subsequently as corrupt politicians or out-of-date and redundant warriors. Such a complex representation of historical events in Africa is important to help expand readerly understandings of colonial, anticolonial, and postcolonial histories.

In several of his novels that deal with revisioning history, Vassanji's characters are haunted by memory, sometimes communal and sometimes individual. But in his latest novel, *Nostalgia*, a tale of speculative fiction set in Toronto at the end of the twenty-first century, a whole society has been built on eradicating painful or violent memories and replacing them with a new version of a life and its pasts. In the novel, Vassanji grapples with the ethics of scientific discovery and asks important questions about immortality, mind renewal, and body renewal. The characters also grapple with the social and economic impact of a limitless life. The novel posits that, in spite of scientific advances, "Leaking Memory, or Nostalgia Syndrome" might exist where memories could refuse to be erased. With the publication of *Nostalgia*, Vassanji has shifted away from his previous work in form and focus, but he is still concerned with issues arising from global movement and the inequitable distributions of power, opportunity, and wealth, alongside a new set of questions about the impact of environmental degradation. As with his other works, however, the recent novel has kept pace with its context of production. The 2016 context of this novel is one in which people are worried about scientific ethics and the environment.

In academic circles, I suspect that Vassanji has long benefitted from the popularization of theories from India and Africa in subaltern studies, postcolonial studies, and subsequently diaspora studies, and globalization studies.[11] But even before postcolonial theory became a standard part of North American university curricula, the study of World Literature Written in English (WLWE) and Commonwealth Literatures helped to bring a selection of the history of Anglo-Indian writing to the attention of non-Indian audiences. That broad-based comparative study tended to focus on a small handful of writers from each community: Raja Rao, R K Narayan, Rabindranath Tagore, and Anita Desai, most predominantly from India. Similarly, African writing was represented in the work of a few: Chinua Achebe, Amos Tutuola, Wole Soyinka, Ngũgĩ wa Thiongo, and Okot p'Bitek. Over the decades, interest transitioned from a fixed geographically framed paradigm to one based on the concept of movement (whether voluntary, exilic, or enforced). Such a transformation of critical frameworks occurred in response to the realities of migration and the resulting multiple constituencies of readers and of writers such as Vassanji, at once African and Indian and Canadian. Earlier categories and theories assuming a fixed nationality have repeatedly proven to be no longer viable or productive.

There is clearly now an international audience hungry for work from the African and Indian diasporas, and this is certainly the case in

Canada. Vassanji's publishers have not been shy to tap into this hunger. It is difficult to say just how much publishers have influenced the trend towards diaspora studies but there is little doubt that they have capitalized on the international desire for writing that touches on multiple locations and multiple histories. Freer global movement of texts and international distribution has led to a greater worldwide accessibility of fiction published in countries like Canada and India as well. However, with multinational publishing conglomerates controlling the major publishing houses (with the Bertelsmann Group controlling Doubleday, Random House, Knopf, and Pantheon, for instance) there has also been increased pressure placed on small independent presses. It is unclear what the impact of this corporatization of publishers has been on a well-established writer like Vassanji. Over the course of his career, Vassanji has worked hard at TSAR and Mawenzi to produce texts that counter the hegemony of these multinationals. He has also consistently chosen to publish with the large companies (as well as TSAR): Canadian (Doubleday, McClelland and Stewart, and Penguin), Indian (Penguin, HarperCollins), American (Knopf, Picador), and British (Heinemann, Canongate). These publishers have been instrumental in showcasing his work as prize worthy in the local and global markets and in nominating his work for international and national awards. The scale and power of Vassanji's particular publishers all but ensure that his work will be advertised, promoted, sold, and read around the world.

It is an interesting offshoot of the long history of globalization and multigenerational diasporic migrations that Vassanji had an Indian publisher—Penguin India—well before he had stepped foot on Indian soil. Indeed, it was the popularity of *The Gunny Sack* (first published in the Heinemann African Writers Series) that first got Vassanji invited to India. Over a decade after he marked himself as a member of the South Asian community in Canada, Vassanji travelled to the land of his grandparents' birth, two generations removed from the land he grew up thinking of as a "distant homeland." It is a remarkable coincidence that the time commonly marked as the watershed for post-liberalization in India roughly corresponds with Vassanji's first visit to the country (1993). His impressions of India from his initial pilgrimage, and from many subsequent visits, are detailed in his memoir *A Place Within: Rediscovering*

India. The memoir tells not only his own story but also outlines an outsider/insider perspective on Indian history. While Vassanji is careful to distance himself from pronouncing on the specifics of the volatile politics of India, particularly the 1993 riots in Bombay, he does not refrain from commentary or judgment on events and individuals. He also tracks, in an unabashedly subjective fashion, his impressions of the impact of liberalization on India over the course of his visits. Again, I turn to the act of self-presentation on Vassanji's website— "Some Personal Notes on the Books"—where he provides meta-commentary on *A Place Within* and his motivation to work on the memoir: "India provokes response and this book is mine. My visits to temple, mosque, church, or synagogue, a beautiful monument or a willfully neglected ruin, an area devastated by mob violence or a friend's house or club, a venerated author or a humble *mukhi*, from the southernmost tip of Kanya Kumari to the misty heights of Shimla, from the viceroys' residence to a Kali temple were all driven by my attempts to understand myself culturally and historically."[12] In this search, he encounters a country in a state of flux (for him it is sometimes terrifying and other times invigorating flux). He also finds that he is at home there. And yet he is also at home elsewhere: in Toronto, in Dar Es Salaam. Home is flexible. In a Canadian interview about *A Place Within*, when Vassanji is asked if he feels caught between two worlds, he answers promptly in the negative: "I went there and I was just Indian. I grew up speaking Indian languages and that helped disguise myself. What I thought was a distant homeland, I realized was very much a part of me. I feel Indian. I also feel African. I feel Canadian. If I was younger I'd feel angst, you know, who am I? But at this age, many countries, it doesn't matter."[13] His recent memoir about growing up in East Africa echoes with stories of comfort in Kenyan and Tanzanian spaces. This is where Vassanji, who finds the boxing in of categories abhorrent, is at his most convincing. The assertion that "it doesn't matter" does not make him postnational but, rather because context still counts, multinational. While he spent his earlier years creating umbrella categories, he is now an unapologetically multinational figure who can be three things at once with no strategic appellations. When literature emerges from such appealing simultaneity, particularly when it is as well-written as Vassanji's work, it is also bound to be well received globally.

JOY KOGAWA

A Long Journey to Mercy: Joy Kogawa's *Gently to Nagasaki*

Irene Sywenky

> The world is filled with unknown stories.
>
> *Gently to Nagasaki* 161

Since the publication of her groundbreaking novel *Obasan* in 1981, Joy Kogawa has been associated with the voice of the Japanese Canadian community and with breaking the silence about its plight as a result of the Dispersal Policy, forcible resettlement and internment during the Second World War. The novel was an important contribution to the movement of redress that resulted in the apology issued by the Mulroney government in 1988 and the historic *Japanese Canadian Redress Agreement*, which acknowledged the social injustice suffered by Japanese Canadians. For her contribution to the Japanese Canadian community and Canadian democratic society she was made a Member of both the Order of Canada and the Order of the Rising Sun. Her most recent work, *Gently to Nagasaki* (2016), is a memoir that sustains a close dialogue with her earlier oeuvre and connects with many of the previously developed themes.

Negotiating between the world of imaginative literary creation and nonfictional writing, the memoir complicates the concept of the autobiographical genre as it engages in a constant movement between Kogawa's well-known novels and the narrative moment of reminiscence. Because all of her earlier writing had attempted to articulate and gain an understanding of real-life traumatic experiences, both in the Japanese Canadian community and in her personal life, the coming of the memoir is not surprising. In her interview with CBC, however, Kogawa admits that she did not exactly plan to write this book: "I was being a leaf in the wind, and the wind blew it that way. I didn't have any choice." "The pen has always been my tool for travelling through thick things" (Hernandez). The memoir becomes a space where she can speak freely, shedding the protective fictional disguise; it also becomes a moment of intense introspective reflection and an integral part of the process of healing.

In both *Obasan* and *Itsuka* Kogawa develops a narrative mode that privileges multiple perspectives, polyphonic voices, and plurifaceted truths; she pursues several narrative itineraries that unfold in a parallel fashion but also remain in continuous dialogue, colliding, intervening, and complicating each other. That is, she uses "postmodern, subversive strategies to challenge traditional ways of thinking about the relationship between history and historical fiction" (Shoenut 479). Through narrative fragmentation and a juxtaposition of different discourses, from documentary and journalistic to lyrical, the writer problematizes a unitary, state-sanctioned history and lays bare the instability and opacity of language. *Gently to Nagasaki* operates in the same narrative mode, developing several thematic lines, mixing various styles, and colliding and reconciling different voices and points of view. The project of the memoir is perhaps anticipated in the attic scene in *Obasan*, where the space of the attic is not only a storage space for material objects from the past, but also a repository of stories and memories that wait to be recovered and retold: "All our ordinary stories are changed in time, altered as much by the present as the present is shaped by the past. Potent and pervasive as a prairie dust storm, memories and dreams seep and mingle through cracks, settling on furniture and into upholstery. Our attics and living-rooms encroach on each other, deep into their invisible places" (*Obasan* 25). The persistence and malleability of memory and the necessity to revisit and reshape the past stories to glean new truths and seek deeper understandings also becomes one of the driving forces in the narrative of *Gently to Nagasaki*: "I see the world as an open book embedded with stories. We hear them if we have ears to hear" (149). The title of the memoir, very appropriately, emphasizes a journey, a slow and careful—even tentative—movement that is quiet and peaceful. Kogawa's shift to the genre of memoir serves as an open declaration of the need—and readiness—to take down the fictional barriers of her previous works. The book brings together the earlier developed themes of speech and silence, home and dislocation, memory, truth, pedophilia and sexual abuse, racism, and social injustice. In the memoir, the repetitive patterns become even more poignantly obvious as the writer pointedly makes connections between her earlier (semi)fictional writing and her life.

The problem of silenced memory and suppressed knowledge, and of inevitable return back to the earlier experience of trauma, constitutes a repetitive pattern that has marked all Kogawa's writing, especially her so-called "novel of memory" (Cook 2007, 54), *Obasan*. If *Obasan*'s narrator Naomi Nakame struggles with reading the past of her violently disrupted childhood, contending that it "does not bear remembering. None of this bears remembering" (54), the memoir also foregrounds the imperative to remember and to speak and at the same time the difficulty or even impossibility of doing so, because the revisitation of trauma is in itself a traumatic moment: "My story is from the belly of the dark. I am forbidden to tell it and commanded to tell it. I am told that to speak is to slay and not to speak is to slay" (47). The insistent return to the earlier experience(s) of trauma is significant for understanding *Gently to Nagasaki*. While most of the scholarship on Kogawa tends to focus on such key works as *Obasan* and, perhaps less often, *Itsuka*, some scholars recognize the importance of considering her other works and the aspects of the creative process that remain in the margins of the Kogawa scholarship. Thus, for example, Benjamin Lefebvre contests the exclusive treatment of *Obasan* and examines the broader context of Kogawa's writing as a pattern of repetition and revision; the latter is particularly important in the case of changes that were made after the initial publication of *Itsuka*, *The Rain Ascends*, as well as the children's story *Naomi's Road*. This point becomes particularly salient in considering *Gently to Nagasaki* as a logical and anticipated development of Kogawa's writing process as an ongoing work of trauma and memory. "If Kogawa's characters are shown moving—to a point—towards reconciliation and forgiveness, why can she not stop writing this story?" (Lefebvre 2010, 155)

The need to write, to revisit and rethink what has already been written drives all of her prose narratives (that are also in dialogue with the themes of the corpus of her earlier poetry, see, e.g., Sywenky) and marks the memoir, a form that speaks openly from a non-fictional perspective, as an inevitable step in the lifelong process of reparation and reconciliation. Arguably, none of her earlier stories leaves the reader with any clear sense of closure, and this factor is indicative of "the extent to which her story of oppression, dispersal, and trauma is *unconcludable*" (Lefebvre 156). The questions about the inherent need to keep telling this story—which, in fact, remains the same story—and the argument on the "unconcludable" nature of the process remain relevant for reading Kogawa's latest work, which engages in an elaborate dialogue with her earlier writings and negotiates the fine line between memory, acknowledgement of crime and injustice, and forgiveness and ponders the possibility of a conclusion.

While the refutation of a finite ending is undoubtedly part of Kogawa's aesthetic as a postmodern writer who recognizes the inherent open-endedness of any discourse and consciously employs postmodern strategies in her novels, the impossibility of a closure can also be seen as the writer's ongoing process of working through the trauma. This duality of her writing—the negation of a possibility of a singular truth but also an incessant and obsessive working towards a possibility of the truth—is ambiguously articulated in the 2003 revised edition of *The Rain Ascends*. Kogawa reflects on story-telling and writing as a universal practice that is inherently grounded in the instability and unreliability of language, while suggesting that the work of memory resists closure, and thus necessitates retroactive revisiting of earlier stories, undoing them and moving beyond what was, at the time, the concluding word: "To every story there is an after-story, and to every life an afterwards. Beyond each punctuation point, each period, are further questionings and more bends in the road ahead than we can imagine" (Kogawa 2003, 192; see also Lefebvre 156). Undoing "each period" and opening up a space for new rereadings, understandings, and truths as a strategy and a memory mechanism is pivotal for approaching *Gently to Nagasaki*.

The narrative of the book lacks a clear organization and deliberately defies any appearance of a linear order. It is a memoir that is also interspersed with epistolary evidence, newspaper clippings, and essayistic reflections on history, politics, and religion. A collection of loosely connected fragments, it underscores the disorderly nature of both writing and memory, while reflecting on the impossibility of separating the deeply private and personal from the social, historical, and political. Its continuity is shaped, on the one hand, through the exploration of the story of the bombing of Nagasaki, where Japan was a victim, and the wartime atrocities of the Japanese Imperial Army, where Japan was a perpetrator; on the other hand, it is also the writer's reflective journey through the Japanese Canadian internment and its aftermath as part of her family's experience—the recovery of her childhood home in Vancouver, lost during the forced relocation of the family to southern Alberta, and dealing with the secret shame of her father's pedophilia. These thematic lines remain relational and interconnected throughout the narrative. The horrors and injustices that people can inflict on each other cannot be separated along personal and historical lines; they collide, intrude and interlock with each other.

The memoir opens with a simple, unembellished retelling of Kogawa's family roots, the wartime events, and the declaration of the twenty-two thousand Japanese Canadians as "enemy aliens" in response to Japan's attack on Pearl Harbor in 1941. The story both connects to what was described in a semiautobiographical way in *Obasan* through a set of fictional characters, and demarcates itself from that past imaginative world by abandoning the poetic style of the novel for a stark declaration of the collective trauma suffered by her community. Another important point of departure for Kogawa is the ironic coincidence that frames the day when the nuclear bomb was dropped on Hiroshima in 1945. August 6, the Feast of Transfiguration, one of the major feasts observed in Christianity, also becomes one of the darkest days humanity will remember. The Japanese word for "transfiguration," through mysterious workings of language, also means "disfiguration," and this duality of meaning, a paradoxical and incomprehensible merging of a sacred beginning and obliteration, becomes part of the many aporias that drive Kogawa's narrative: a paradoxical simultaneity of being Canadian and non-Canadian during the wartime years, of being silenced but also compelled to speak, of being a victim and a perpetrator, of negotiating ambivalent truths and untruths.

In her narrative, Kogawa engages in a hermeneutic quest where she becomes a reader of her own earlier writing and the metafiction of her memories, past and present. She reflects on the question whether the absent mother in *Obasan* in fact signified the absent God and wonders at the stoic nature of her people: the Japanese Canadians who worked the beet fields of Alberta and the Japanese who heroically persevered in the aftermath of the events in Fukushima. If Kogawa translated and interpreted her own life experiences through the lens of her fictional worlds, as a writer, an activist, and a person, she in turn was also created by other stories and books. She traces the many influences that other people's writing had both on her creative life and her personal worldview. Muriel Kitagawa's *This Is My Own* had a seminal impact on Kogawa's writing *Obasan*, especially in her shaping of the character of Aunt Emily. A journalist and a political activist, Kitagawa became a model of an unwavering truth-seeker and a strong voice in the landscape of political silence. Much later in her life, Kogawa attends the performance of *A Nanking Winter* by playwright Marjorie Chan, which also leads her to Iris Chang's earlier book, *The Rape of Nanking: The Forgotten Holocaust of World War II*. This chance encounter changes her view of Japan's history. The complex entanglements of history and imaginative literary worlds, the two-way trajectories between life and fiction, are part of the meaning-making and deeper understanding that shape this narrative journey.

The theme of trauma and the ambivalent complexity of the victim/victimizer dichotomy is one of the running threads in the memoir that brings together its multiple narratives. Kogawa's reflections on Japan revolve around her personal ties to that country and her travels there, as well as the two events that scarred the country forever, each in a different way—the two holocausts of Nanking and Nagasaki, the horrors of which defy reason and human understanding and resist articulation through language. Kogawa moves between the sketches of the different human agents who, in their own way, contributed to the obliteration of this city—the pilot who dropped the bomb, the priest, Father George Zabelka, who said prayers over the Hiroshima and Nagasaki missions, and the saintly figure of Dr Takashi Nagai, who meticulously recorded the atomic illness in survivors and developed new treatments to ease their sufferings. At the time Nagasaki was a western-oriented city, a centre of science and research, a scene of dynamic intellectual life, and a long-standing seat of Christianity in Asia; ironically, the bombing of Nagasaki almost completely destroyed its community of Christians at the hands of their western counterparts, the community that could not be obliterated through a long history of persecution in Japan. In the aftermath of the Holocaust of WWII, when "the search for meaning became heinous," Kogawa nonetheless "cannot accept meaninglessness as an answer to Nagasaki" (16). The unspeakable horrors of annihilation have to be articulated, and the broken silence of Father Zabelka on the fortieth anniversary of the bombings was an important step toward a possibility of forgiveness. However "feeble" this step was, according to him, the public acknowledgement of the unspeakable past was "the essential step in the process of repentance and reconciliation: admission of error, admission of guilt" (23).

Kogawa's discovery of Marjorie Chan's play and Iris Chang's book turned a new page in her understanding of Japan's history. Chang's reconstruction of the atrocities of the 1937-38 massacre of Nanking at the hands of the Japanese Imperial Army, at the time largely unknown to the West, brought back the recollection of being an "enemy alien" and the feelings of "deep shame" and "deep horror." Kogawa's traumatic memories of her childhood and the racist labels she received persisted through her ambivalent associations with being Japanese, which haunted her for years ("I worked to erase any identification with the unmentionable country,"164)). Chang's narrative was simultaneously compelling, profoundly shocking, and repulsive in its depiction of horror: "I could not continue reading. I could not stop reading. I could not will away her words. I could not turn my mind's eye from the pictures" (166). Kogawa insists that any nation's recognizing the dark pages in its history and lifting the silence on the past mistakes, whether Canada or Japan, is the only path towards reconciliation and moving forward. Japan's dual narrative as both a victim and a perpetrator of horrific wartime crimes, and the many negotiations and retellings of this narrative from different ideological and political perspectives, cannot obfuscate the central truth about the past tragedies. In her conversation with Marjorie Chan, she questions why there are so "few stories about Asia on the world stage" (163);

however troubling and controversial, some stories always find their way out, through “blood-veined stones,” the victims’ bodies, or forgotten and neglected archives.

Perhaps the most controversial and ambivalent as well as the most personal issue that Kogawa addresses in her memoir is her father’s pedophilia and abuse of dozens of young boys, which was exposed during his postwar trip to Okinawa as an Anglican minister. Even though this issue remains central to her narrative journey, the writer approaches the painful subject almost hesitantly in Part II, in a nonlinear time-space, weaving in her discussions with a psychiatrist on the subject of sexual abuse and conversations with close friends. It was a terrifying experience, inflicted on Kogawa when she was still a teenager and could not comprehend fully its gravity. After months of a gloomy and mysterious mood in the family, the two words uttered one day by her mother—“sex” and “boys”—changed Kogawa’s subsequent years: “They [the words] fell into the forest of my mind and lay there through the springtime of my life, through summer drought and into winter snows, words to be forgotten. Although they remained unseen they changed my life irrevocably” (90). She suffered from severe bouts of nausea, and, with time, the trauma became more pervasive, as she thought of the many young victims of Gordon Nakayama. In seeking her own understanding of what had happened and retrospectively analyzing her own way of responding to it, in reading her reading of the past Kogawa collapses the concept of the unproblematic unitary truth and questions the possibility of a clear, unbiased position:

> The truth was that the person I loved and admired more than anyone in the world, the one with whom I most identified, the one who told stories and made life fun, who wept and laughed and sang, who was good and did not give up, the one in whom I could see no wrong and who saw no wrong in me, my father, a visionary and charismatic priest in the Anglican Church, a man who had served his scattered flock and his people without letup: my adored father was a paedophile. (52)

Kogawa says that the original publication of *The Rain Ascends* in 1995, where she addresses the subject of sexual abuse by a priest, brought about a new state of health: “The secret shame in my family was out, even if only in fictional form, and a lifelong sickness ended" (68), even though it was short-lived. She speaks with brutal honesty about her initial inability to acknowledge the scope and gravity of her father's crimes and see him as a perpetrator, which stirs animosity among her friends and weakens her bonds with the community, who demand an official recognition of the crimes he had committed and a harsher condemnation. While spending time with her father in the later years of his life and being with him through his terminal illness, she discovers that he was briefly sexually molested as a child, and so an abuser was also an abused. Deciding to break her own silence and denial, she carefully and hesitantly speaks with some of her father's victims about what had happened. What she discovers shocks and cripples her emotionally. This becomes, she writes, her "Nagasaki, a barren place of no light" (158), a realm of the unspeakable, a void beyond language and meaning. Towards the end of the memoir, Kogawa recounts her 2009 trip to Japan that culminated in visiting her father's birthplace. Remembering him as someone she carried with her throughout her life, there, "among the dead who had known and loved him," she hoped to lay down "[her] burden and leave [her] father in the care of his own" (201).

In negotiating the many terrains of trauma in her narrative, Kogawa keeps returning to the experience of horror that anchors her memories of childhood resettlement as well as later dislocations, both physical and emotional. The insistent references to horror and its pattern of repetition constitutes an important thematic element that connects Kogawa's memoir to her earlier work. As it was noted by Turcotte, with specific reference to *Obasan*, there is a certain gothic quality that informs the narrative: "Her account makes frightening reading because it demonstrates the fragility of rights that should have been taken for granted—of belonging, of citizenship, of liberty, and justice. These rights were extinguished overnight and re-written in the name of undisguised racism. Identity was destabilized. The experience seems straight out of a gothic novel—except that it was true" (Turcotte 82). This Gothicism, the unthinkable terror of a spiraling collapse of all that is rational and human, permeates many pages of *Gently to Nagasaki*. When talking about Iris Chang's book describing Japan's war atrocities, Kogawa wonders about the author's process of research and working on the manuscript, its publication and the ensuing controversy, and later her suicide. Kogawa wonders if "she couldn't get the horrors out of her mind" (162). Chang's experience surely resonated with Kogawa, who tried coping with many profoundly terrifying revelations on both individual and communal planes, and both personal and historical: the horror of discovering and dealing with her father's past; the "horror writ large on the world stage"; and the "vast, unthinkable unseeing and the fraying of more bonds with friends" (161) that followed the disclosure of her father's crimes.

One of the important questions raised by the trauma theorist Cathy Caruth in her recent conversation with the renowned psychiatrist Bessel van der Kolk is whether the healing process is about "healing the self, or healing the culture" (166). While van der Kolk remained skeptical about the subject of culture, which is grounded in the realm of politics, and about the possibility of changing the political landscape (167), he at the same time emphasized the importance of the "relational aspect" of language in the process of healing: "language . . . gives you a voice and provides a possibility of being in touch with the rest of the human race. Language at least offers the possibility that people will acknowledge what has happened to you, and believe you" (163). Speaking within a public space of a published narrative does precisely that: it allows one to be heard by "the rest of the human race," and in *Gently to Nagasaki* Kogawa makes herself heard through a voice that is caring, loving, and compassionate.

Suggesting the possibility of a conclusion and a closure would mean to simplify what Kogawa undertakes in her memoir and what the deeply introspective process of self-reflection and writing meant to her, but her candid conversation with the reader anticipates acknowledgement and belief. In an earlier essay, "Is There a Just Cause?" presented to the Canadian Caucus on Human Rights in 1983, Kogawa emphasizes the importance of the public word and public recognition of past injustices. Revisioning and rewriting the history "[i]n this our not-yet-completed storytelling time" (162) becomes an integral part of addressing the past traumas and restoring trust. Through words that are still meaningful and possibly even more important and relevant today, Kogawa asserts that "the energy for healing, for reconciliation, for forgiveness and for mutuality are endlessly . . . accessible to us" (162). *Gently to Nagasaki* is a beautiful narrative that, among other things, is about the power of the story-telling moment. If there is a possibility of closure, it is in the journey itself and the gentle movement forward to understanding, truth, trust, and forgiveness.

SHAUNA SINGH BALDWIN

Gendered Violence and Feminist Interventions in Shauna Singh Baldwin's *The Selector of Souls*

Asma Sayed

> She is defined and differentiated with reference to man and not with reference to her; she is the incidental, the inessential. He is the subject, he is the Absolute, she is the other.
>
> Simone de Beauvoir, *The Second Sex*

Literary texts can offer understandings of the power structures within which violence operates, for example the structures of race, class, gender, and ability. In this essay, I will examine how gender-based violence is indicative of broader sociocultural issues, including rape culture, in Shauna Singh Baldwin's novel, *The Selector of Souls* (2013). Baldwin is an award-winning Canadian author of Indian origin with a number of books to her credit, including three novels, namely, *What the Body Remembers* (2000), *The Tiger Claw* (2004), and *The Selector of Souls*; two short story collections, *English Lessons and Other Stories* (1996) and *We Are Not in Pakistan* (2007); and a collection of essays, *Reluctant Rebellions* (2016). In addition, she has published poems, essays, and fiction in literary magazines and anthologies.

Baldwin's fictions are female-inclusive narratives. *The Selector of Souls*, set in postcolonial India, engages with various forms of aggression against women, including rape, domestic and sexual violence, physical and emotional trauma, sex determination, female foeticide, male favouritism, and the exploitation of older women. These issues are placed within the context of religious orthodoxy, at times fanaticism, encompassing the 1984 massacre of Sikhs in Delhi following the assassination of Prime Minister Indira Gandhi by her Sikh bodyguards, the demolition of the Babri Mosque in 1992, and the role of the Roman Catholic Church in curbing women's rights to their bodies.

Through the intertwining stories of four lead female characters, who operate at the intersections of ethnic, religious, class and caste conflicts, Baldwin presents the lived realities of women as second-class citizens and the abuses they endure. Her women are of different ages and social circumstances. The marginalization they face is wide-ranging, and their stories unfold as they resist socioeconomic and cultural hierarchies and expectations, disrupting Indian patriarchal hegemonies. Despite abuse, or rather, because of it, these characters chart their own paths, seeking justice for themselves and other women; but the law is either not on their side or takes too long to serve them justice. The failure of the system leads to these characters resorting to desperate measures. In this essay, I argue that not only do the actions of the female characters serve as feminist interventions within the text, but also, Baldwin's exposé of violence against women through her fictional characters itself serves as an interventionist project.

There is a recognized lineage of South Asian women's writing focusing on women's issues. Their attempts have been both criticized as presenting a narrative of victimhood (see Mohanty et al; Jia; and Ghosh and Bose) and valorized as representing the realities of women's lived experiences. In the twentieth century, writers such as Ismat Chughtai, Nayantara Sehgal, Anita Desai, Bapsi Sidhwa, Kiran Desai, Monica Ali, and Anita Rau Badami have all focused on women's issues, drawing attention to the subordinate positioning of women in South Asian sociocultural, legal, political, and domestic arenas. (See Tharu and Lalita for a detailed history of women's writing in India.) Much of Partition literature has focused on the violence that accompanied the end of the British Raj and the partitioning of India, especially sexual violence against women.

Baldwin's novel focuses mainly on the lives of two women: Damini and Anu. Damini is an older Hindu woman, a poor maid who works for an upper-class Sikh woman simply called Mem-saab in the novel. Anu is a young Hindu-Christian woman who leaves her violence-filled married life, sends her daughter to live with her cousin in Canada, and becomes a nun. Anu eventually leaves her Christian missionary work and charts out her own life. We are also introduced to the intricacies of the lives of many other women in the book, especially Mem-saab and Goldina, the latter a Dalit convert to Christianity. All these women face one or another form of violence, but by banding together they are able to fight their oppressors and counter the larger cultural bias against women.

The novel is set in northern India, mainly in the metropolis of New Delhi and the small village named Gurkot in the Himalayas. The women, whether from upper-class families or poor homes, suffer similarly. Violence against women is pervasive in India, as it is in many societies across the globe, and takes many forms. Watt and Zimmerman explain:

> In practice, the term "violence against women" encompasses an array of abuses targeted at women and girls, ranging from sex-selective abortion to the abuse of elder women. The term includes geographically or culturally specific forms of abuse such as genital mutilation, dowry deaths, acid throwing, and honour killings (the murder of women who have allegedly brought shame to their family), as well as forms of violence that are prevalent worldwide such as domestic violence and rape. (1232)

In India, female foeticide and infanticide, dowry deaths, sexual assaults, and domestic violence all emanate from centuries-old beliefs about women's social, cultural, and religious roles.

Baldwin illustrates, through the character of Anu and the abuses she endures at the hands of her husband, how the patriarchal structures are reinforced to maintain a certain social order. Anu, the trophy wife of a businessman, Vikas Kohli, is tortured physically, emotionally, and psychologically. She is the mother of a teenage girl, Chetna, who is the result of an incident of marital rape. Reports by United Nations and other organizations show that intimate-partner violence is one of the most common forms of violence against women. When she is introduced in the novel, the reader learns of her life in a big mansion, hiding the abuse that she faces on a daily basis: "Anu lives in this Taj Mahal of a home with her husband and in-laws. With a cook to help her, with servants to clean, to wash her and tidy her cupboards . . . She can get a facial and have her makeup done at the Taj Palace Hotel whenever she needs to cover up a swollen or purpling eye" (41). It is clear that her husband, Vikas, expects only compliance from Anu: "All Vikas's decisions are right. Even those to come. He is corrective and combative with waiters in five-star hotel restaurants, ushers at movie theatres, his personal barber. He admonishes his gardener, his security guard, his drivers—whom he now calls chauffeurs. No one challenges him, no one protests, so he brings his public imperiousness home" (43). He treats Anu no differently from the way he treats his servants. But he also wants from Anu a male child; he "[prodded] her to produce the son he needed to carry on his family name" (46). But Anu does not want children. Enraged by her denial, Vikas rapes her. Anu's attempts to file a complaint against him are unsuccessful, the police convinced that incidents like marital rape "don't happen in India. Only abroad" (46). Every time Anu sees Chetna, she is reminded that their daughter "was born of Vikas's disbelief that any woman would not want a child. She was born of violence" (46). For Vikas, raping his wife and regularly physically abusing her are part of married life. The concept of marital rape does not exist in the Kohli household. Vikas's mother does not think that her son is capable of rape; according to her, if Vikas did rape Anu, she may have called it upon herself by refusing to comply with his demands, a standard blame-the-victim narrative typical to patriarchal understanding of gender-based violence. Thus, Anu has no recourse, familial, legal or social. As a wife she is expected to be sexually available to her husband regardless of her wishes.

Women are considered the guardians of traditions, morals, and family reputations. Therefore, a woman herself is the property of her family, and specifically the patriarch. After a period of continued violence, when Anu decides to seek divorce, her uncle, Sharad, who raised her, is hysterically against the idea. He worries not only about her future, but also about his own social standing. He asserts to Anu that she is simply passing through a phase, and all women should learn to compromise. He advises her to have another child, "[p]regnancy will cure [her] of these . . . these hysterical wishes" (95). As I have argued elsewhere (See Sayed, 2016), South Asian culture, much like other cultures, glamorizes motherhood, and the maternal role is considered central to the identity of women. Jasjit K Sangha and Tahira Gonsalves argue:

> In South Asian culture, motherhood has historically held significant meaning and women's reproductive abilities have been celebrated, through rituals performed in ancient India, writings in religious texts in Buddhism, Hinduism, Islam and Sikhism, and traditional practices of matriarchy in some communities. However, along with this reverence came terms and conditions, steeped in patriarchy, that defined how women should mother. Most notably, that women should aspire motherhood within a heterosexual marriage, and as mothers, they should be sacrificial and devoted to their families. (2)

Thus, in the novel, Uncle Sharad believes that if Anu gives birth to a male child, her in-laws will treat her better and she will not need to leave her husband. Anu's mother (who has given him Anu to raise) is also against the idea of Anu leaving her husband: "I have to bear the shame . . . because you've made your father look so bad. I hope you realize what you've accomplished" (98). Divorces are still a matter of shame in many Indian households. Although Anu is mistreated by her husband, her relatives would prefer that she put up with the abuse and continue her marriage. The attitude of Uncle Sharad is all too common. Anu, not wanting to burden her uncle and aunt or her parents, decides to send her daughter, Chetna, to her cousin in Canada and herself becomes a nun. In her missionary work through St Anne's Convent, she goes through many hoops while learning about women's lives. But even while she is at the Convent she is pursued by Vikas who, once he finds out where she lives, stalks her and once again physically attacks her. The trauma of living under the constant threat of violence is intense, and Anu begins to sleep with a knife under her pillow. Her trauma is indicative of a broad issue within Indian society: when women choose to leave their abusive situations, their safety is compromised, and there are no social networks to protect them, not even the family.

Religious institutions do not always provide refuge to battered women. As Anu learns more about the orthodoxy of the Church, and figures out that it does not quite provide the sanctuary that she needs, she leaves. She has recognized that religious ideologies do not help further women's rights; if anything, she thinks, they put constraints on women. When she decides to leave the nunnery, and refuses to run a clinic, she tells Sister Imaculata, her superior:

> I'm no longer the right person for it . . . I fear I will recommend birth control pills to women like Goldina. I now feel abortion should be available to women who need it because of rape or any other reason. I think a woman must own her own body all the way to the moment a child takes its first breath and gains consciousness at birth. And I believe Damini's daughter Leela should have been able to get an early abortion even though I could not have brought myself to have one. (473)

She has concluded that women's liberation will happen one woman at a time, and certainly not through institutions abiding by age-old beliefs and customs. She tries to find her identity—as a wife, mother, daughter, daughter-in-law, nun, and nurse; eventually, she finds a space for herself and becomes a nurse in a hospital. But her independence comes at a cost.

Anu must take her destiny into her own hands. Without options, she even fantasizes about killing Vikas, because that seems to be the only way out of her situation. When seeking legal advice for her divorce, she asks the lawyer: "How long would I spend in jail if . . . if I kill him?" (67) Towards the end of the novel, she actually gets a chance to fulfill her fantasy. Vikas gets injured in a terrorist attack, and it happens that he is admitted to the same hospital where Anu works. When his new wife comes to visit him, Anu sees that she has bruises on her arms. Vikas's violence has simply been redirected to another woman. Figuring that men like him, for whom violence is a means of asserting their power over a woman, do not change, she decides to act. Her intervention here, on behalf of the second wife, might be considered problematic: she administers a lethal injection to Vikas. She goes on to justify her action: "What is right action? What is dharma? Is it not to go to the defense of a woman whose soul is being crushed, who cannot act for herself? Is it not to do what should be done for justice to prevail? Not the law—justice!" (540) She has come to the conclusion that she "must overcome conscience and empathy to become a selector of souls, and do what must be done" (540).

Her act of murder is an intervention into the abuses of women and the discourses that silence them.

Baldwin presents yet another horrifying intervention through the story of Damini. If Anu's act of murder shakes the reader, Damini's actions are equally, if not more, shocking. Damini, a maid who works for Mem-saab, navigates through the world of son-preference and sex-selective abortions. She has a son, Suresh, who works as a school teacher and is close to Hindu fundamentalists. Damini's daughter, Leela, is married to a trucker, who is dying of AIDS. When Mem-saab dies, Damini has no choice but to go and seek shelter with her daughter, even though living with a daughter is considered a huge taboo. As the novel opens, Damini arrives at Leela's house in Gurkot, where she learns that Leela is pregnant; subsequently she tries to help Leela abort her baby, in her belief that Leela cannot afford one more child. When her home remedies fail, and Leela gives birth to a daughter, Damini kills her in order to save Leela from the trial of feeding another daughter.

Damini's actions are rooted in the internalization of discriminatory patriarchal practices. Power imbalances are structured in such a way that a female child is discriminated against soon after conception. Ultrasound technologies, one of the focuses of Baldwin's novel, are used, illegally in India, to determine the sex of the fetus. Although India has criminalized sex determination, each year thousands of female fetuses are aborted, which has led to an imbalance in the male-female ratio in the population. According to a report in the medical journal *Lancet*, in the two decades following the 1990s, some ten million girls may have been lost due to sex-selective abortions, and the "girl-deficit" was "more common among educated women." The desire for male children is rooted in age-old cultural beliefs that favour sons. This stigmatization of females furthers the violence against them. In the wake of the much-publicized Nirbhaya gang-rape case of December 2012, many young women took to the streets to protest. The police action in response was brutal. Thus, while India is becoming more aware of its records on gender equality, it still remains one of the least desirable places for women to live in. Watts and Zimmerman confirm that "women's unequal status helps to create their vulnerability to violence, which in turn fuels the violence perpetuated against them" (1232). And Cruz and Rao remind us that "violence has been a central object of feminist analysis and theorization, precisely because it has been the unifying ground for much feminist activism" (1). While it may be simplistic to describe the experiences of Indian women from different classes, castes, and religious categories by a singular narrative, the exposure to violence in multiple forms does bring these women out together in their resistance.

Damini, too, eventually gets her distorted sense of justice, but before she gets to that level of understanding, she justifies the infanticide by saying: "*This is my role in the movie of Leela's Life*" (emphasis in the original, 9). She saw the sadness at the birth of a girl in Damini's eyes and asked herself, "Did this child dream, in its soft cocoon, that it would enter the world to such a chorus of sights, tears and recrimination? Does it see, as it opens its eyes for the first time, that condemned look on Leela's face?" (235) Damini examines the child, wiping "between its legs, looking for a penis," but she is disappointed. She asks herself, "Why did this atman incarnate? Only the gods know. Jee doesn't ask for birth. The purush-energy of fathers like Chunilal pulls it into existence. And so this soul came, bringing all the desires of a being. Because it became a girl, along with it came all the expectations and demands of her someday husband and family" (8). Clearly, Damini thinks that it is the male energy that facilitates reproduction, and her first worry is about the baby's marriage many years later. She realizes that raising this baby, this soul "that has mistakenly entered this world" would mean a lifetime of saving for her dowry (9). The birth of a girl child is a message of doom for the child, who will be punished, and for her parents, who will raise her to give her away someday to her husband (9). Damini wonders:

> What terrible deeds must this soul have done in a past life, to now be punished by taking form as a girl. What will she face but suffering that leads to more suffering. Did this girl know, as she grew according to some intricate plan of the gods, that her incredibly complex form is yet inadequate? Does this girl feel that she has become the node of sorrow, that she is born disabled by her womanhood? Does she know yet, from the

> sad melody of speech heard in her mother's belly, just how unwanted she is? (236)

Being born a girl is the worst of fates for a human being. Therefore Damini kills the baby, "push[ing] the tobacco into the tiny mouth" (9). She believes that the time is not right for a girl to be born; she prays to goddess Anamika Devi: "*Release this atman, girl-body. Let it return to the place that continues long before and long after this world. Let it take shape when this world is a better place for girls*" (emphasis in the original, 9).

After this event, in order to support herself, Damini assists women in getting sex-selective abortions; she takes pregnant women to illegal abortion clinics and accepts a commission for each referral. She believes she is doing this for a greater cause. She "feels like Narada on the path of the devotee: she is a pair of ears again, listening to women. Helping women do as they want" (216). It is interesting to note that she herself lives with the guilt of being born a girl; her mother self-immolated and "lit her own funeral pyre" after Damini was born and her father decided to take a second wife who would bear him sons: "And I knew then, that I killed my mother by taking shape, entering the world when I did. Couldn't I have waited? Why didn't I listen to her wishes and die in her womb? Couldn't I have gone to some other woman and not added to the burdens of a woman who already had four daughters?" (230) The cycle of violence continues generation after generation as women internalize the patriarchal customs and beliefs passed on to them.

At the same time, Shauna Singh offers a critique of the institution of motherhood. Mothers are too permissive with the boys they raise, thereby concretizing historically unjust social relations. Damini, as a mother herself, continuously ignores her son Suresh's many criminal activities. She sees him on TV demolishing the Babri Mosque along with a mob of some 200,000 people. Although "shame churned in Damini's stomach like the milky ocean that birthed the world," she's never confronted him. She saves money for him, convinced that he is a good man: "But he's a good son—he attends prayer and exercise classes of the Rashtriya Swayam Sewak every morning. And he doesn't shout at his mother . . . " (24) Suresh is a follower of Hindu fundamentalist groups, to which he donates most of the money she gives him, and he participates in sectarian violence, yet her mother-love for her son always gets the better of her.

Suresh was Goldina's rapist. Being a low-caste Dalit woman converted to Christianity makes Goldina more vulnerable to sexual violence, especially during times of religious tensions among communities. As Ritu Menon and Kamla Bhasin have argued, "the dramatic episodes of violence against women during communal riots bring to the surface, savagely and explicitly, familiar forms of sexual violence—now charged with a symbolic meaning that serves as indicator of the place women's sexuality occupies in the all-male, patriarchal arrangement of gender relations, between religious or ethnic communities" (41). When Goldina's husband refuses to carve a statue of Savarkar, a Hindu Nationalist icon, for Suresh, he threatens revenge. He corners Goldina the next day and rapes her "to teach her a lesson" (385). Goldina is left bleeding and crying on the pavement. When her husband Samuel finds out about the rape, he beats her up as "he could not beat the teacher" (385). While Goldina is multiply marginalized, Damini's initial refusal to acknowledge and believe Goldina's story stems from her own upper-caste attitudes. Thus, the novel complicates the matter by showing that women themselves may at times become agents of patriarchy, an example of victims turned into oppressors. Some of the choices that Damini makes are horrific and they haunt her, but who is to judge her actions, which she perceives as altruistic? Her interventions, as misplaced as they are, in her mind are done for the betterment of women's lives. It is only after she meets Anu, who herself is struggling with her own interventionist practices, that Damini realizes the long-term consequences of her actions and sets on a path of change. She starts a women's group; and she learns to appreciate her granddaughter Kamna, who becomes the family's next breadwinner. In allowing Kamna to drive her father's truck to earn money, Damini paves a path for the next generation of women to become economically independent and move on to their liberation.

Shauna Singh Baldwin's *The Selector of Souls* both displays and challenges the long-standing patriarchal arrangements in India. The novel exposes multiple structures that not only enable violence against women, but also make it a day-to-day part of India's social fabric; it serves in addition as a medium of "remembering and recording [the] experience and struggles" of women (Mohanty 77). On one hand, Anu is highly educated and married into a rich family. Damini, on the other, is a poor, uneducated maid who has spent much of her life working for other people. Both are victims of a patriarchal society that marginalizes women in myriad ways. Vikas, Suresh, and later Aman are men who empower themselves and subordinate the women in their lives through aggression and violence. Ultimately the women take control of their own destinies and form a sister-bond to help each other fight against their oppression. That is a positive outcome. But in the process these survivor women have paid a high price: Mem-saab commits suicide; Damini kills her granddaughter; Anu kills her ex-husband; and Goldina gives her baby up for adoption.

Notes

"This dock is my dock": Dionne Brand's Room of Light

1. In the sense suggested by the text of "against the turn, against the furrow" (Verso 7).

2. "Must I be explicit—the human—it exists in the world. But it is occupied," the clerk explains (Verso 11).

3. Other writers Brand mentions as part of her political-cultural formation are Lorca, Neruda, Saramago and Carpentier. See Brand, Verso 7.

4. In "Listening to a Listening: The Disruptive Jazz Poetics of Dionne Brand's *Ossuaries* (A Call Towards Freedom)," Paul Watkins provides a cogent reading of this long poem as "an extended jazz solo."

5. See also "I leave my house and immediately my body is ripped from me to enact some colonial idyll. I look out a window. I wash my hands. I touch my eyebrows. I am on the eternal other stage. My teeth are examined. My arms are sized up. My hips measured. I pull my head in from the window. I try to hide. It's useless." (Verso 15.1)

6. Interestingly enough, the motto of the Anthropology pavilion at the World's Columbian Exposition (Chicago 1893) was "To see is to know." See Blanchard et al, *Human Zoos, Science and Spectacle in the Age of Colonial Empires,* 1.

7. "On Some Motifs in Baudelaire," Benjamin, *Illuminations*, 157-202.

8. This quote refers to slavery and the slave trade. In this verso the author evokes her visit to the Museum of London Docklands. On this occasion she discovered that a certain John Brand was the captain of a slave ship. Hence an (unsuccessful) research in the archives to trace this clue further.

9. It would be interesting to pursue how another notion explored by Benjamin, the phantasmagoria of reified human labour, is given another twist when Kamau Brathwaite speaks of "the warped fantastic environment of our lives": a condition, or consciousness, that the author acknowledges as her own (Verso 13.1). But

also other concepts of Benjamin's dialectical materialism, such as the debris of history, or the crisis of the humanistic concept of freedom, might be explored in this contrapuntal light. More explicitly, Baudrillard's theorization of the "hyperreal" is related to Ellison's "absurdism": "The protagonist lived in a world as I of the absurd, but somehow everyone believed it was credible. Just summon Baudrillard here if you like. The hyperreal was hyperreal already. For us." (Verso 21.4)

10. I am resorting here to Richard Kearney's explanation of the use of this term in structural and post-structural linguistics ("What is Diacritical Hermeneutics?" 3), but actually in an unpublished article ("An Ars Poetica from the Blue Clerk"), Brand herself, as Leslie Sanders points out, proposes poetry as a "diacritic for narratives of Black life." She refers, more specifically, to the way in which diacritical marks change "the sound, tone, or meaning of certain words." (Leslie Sanders, "Austin Clarke's Poetic Turn," 66). Moreover, a section of the Index is precisely titled "The Diacritical."

11. In Verso 1.1.01, the author reminisces about her first library, that is, her grandfather's logbook, where he logged "hundredweight of copra, pounds of chick feed and manure . . . the nuisance of heliconia; the depth of two rivers; the length of a rainy season." She also recalls the "liquid hand" of the sea, that "would turn a liquid page each eight seconds" and the organic styli, that the children would call pens, washed up onto the beach.

12. Ibid. In *The Blue Clerk*, such "racist alphabets," in so far as they are "at the core, a construction of the zoo," are deemed so powerful as to infect the vocabulary itself of resistance: "Even the language that we used to combat the more awful ailments, even that can be turned inward on itself . . . So you are dying in their etymology." (Verso 15.1)

13. Christina Sharpe comments on the entire verso in her powerful "analytic" of slavery's yet unresolved unfolding. See Sharpe, *In the Wake. On Blackness and Being*, 25-27.

14. Merleau-Ponty argues this point with regard to paintings. See Merleau-Ponty, *Signs*, 44.

15. On John Coltrane's style, see Anderson, *This is Our Music*, 71.

16. On the other hand, colours like orange and green denote and connote a more private, silent language of omission, or "withdrawal," that flashes out in Verso 2.1, referred to in the Index as "the potions deleted from the Versos." Here orange appears as "a column of orange air" that the author saw as a child while in Verso 44 orange is part of the "gradatios" of the author's "decades of emergency" recorded by the clerk, who has retained "the sense of orange." Likewise, here the sound of a window "falling shut" replaces the visual perception of the "green window held open with a stick"of Verso 43. Here appears, as well, "the escarpment of a yellow house dividing the world," evoked in Verso 4 and, indirectly, Verso 50. In Verso 2.1 "yellow," as pure colour, is once again connected to what the child saw. Retrospectively (on the clerk's request), the author specifies its particular tonality, as she does with green.

17. For example, in Verso 2.5, the author "depicts" the flight across the four Bocas del Dragon of her great grandmother Angelina as if it were the subject of a

water colour. In Verso 3.1, the city of Toronto is compared to a painting by Romare Bearden or Basquiat.

18. This is a quote from Merleau-Ponty (*Signs* 46) but in an interview it is Brand herself who says, with reference to *Ossuaries*: "Suggests lyric, but is like, what? That shakes up sound" ("To Promote Statements," 10).

19. See Ornette Coleman, "Prime Time for Harmolodics," 54-55.

20. This quote is from Verso 4, which consists of a riveting re-evocation of an epiphany that occurred to the nine-year-old author. Recounted by means of repetition, variation, restatement and progressive amplification of the initial syntactic unit, the impact of this "diacritical" moment of revelation ("it came over me that I was not going to live here all my life, that I was going away and never returning some day") is also visually orchestrated around a "yellow washed house" contemplated from the top of a street.

21. In Bertolt Brecht's sense that "a thought must be crude in order to come into its own in action." See Arendt, "Introduction." Walter Benjamin, *Illuminations*, 15.

Landscape and Diasporic Citizenship(s) in Ramabai Espinet's *The Swinging Bridge* and *Nuclear Seasons*

1. In this essay, I do not retrace the beaten paths detailing the peripheralization of hyphenated new-Canadian authors from the central debates on Canadian literature. For this see New 1985, 1992, 1994; Deer 1999; Genetsch 2007; Cuder-Domínguez et al. 2011; and Kim and Lee 2016, inter alia). Rather, my focus pinpoints an aspect of Ramabai Espinet's engagement of landscape ecologies of identity to define Indo-Caribbean politics of identity both in the Caribbean and in Canada. Indubitably, Espinet's work gravitates toward certain elemental Indo-Trinidadian personal and group cultural, political, ethnic identities (Solbaic 229-231; Ramraj 78). This, Hall (257), and Brah (126) argue, is reflective of a strategic maneuvering against an earlier hegemonic Afro-Trinidadian narrative of multiculturalism in a pre/post-independence Trinidad (Solbaic 44-45)

Cecil Foster's *Sleep on, Beloved*: Reflections on Afro-Caribbean Immigrant Existence in Toronto

1. Following is a list of novels, by no means exhaustive, that could be helpful to readers wishing to put Foster's vision into the broader perspective of immigrant novels by non-White immigrants about Canada: Austin Clarke's *The Meeting Point* (1967), *Storm of Fortune* (1973), *The Bigger Light* (1975); M G Vassanji's *No New Land* (1991); Neil Bisssoondath's *A Casual Brutality* (1988); Althea Prince's *Loving This Man* (2001); M. Nourbese Philip' *Harriet's Daughter* (1988); Makeda Silvera's *The Heart Does not Bend* (2002); Dionne Brand's *Any Place, Not Here* (1996) and *What We all Long For* (2005); Nalini Warriar's *The Enemy Within* (2005); Arnold Harrichand Itwaru's *Home and Back* (2001); Paula Aird's *What*

Goes Around . . . (2004); Max Dorsinville's *Erzulie Loves Shango* (1998); and H. Nigel Thomas's *Behind the Face of Winter* (2001). Most of these works depict the psychic cost the new life exacts, and in most the costs neutralize the gains, but a few—Aird's, Silvera's, Itwaru's, for example—have positive balances in the assets column of the immigration ledger.

2. Arnold Itwaru argues that "the stranger categorized in the name and label 'immigrant' is already invented as 'immigrant,' a distinctiveness which is also anonymous upon arrival. This person is no longer the bearer of another history, but has now become a particular *other*, the bearer of a label invented by the 'host.'" (1990, 13-14).

3. Here Ona's words echo statements made by Dionne Brand (2001, 90-91) and Nourbese Philip (1992, 10), two Caribbean-Canadian writers, who affirm that the educational curriculum in Trinidad seemed designed to prepare them for emigration. Foster too extensively analyzes this subject in his memoir *Island Wings* and explores it via fiction in *No Man in the House*, a novel which he restricts to a Barbados setting.

4. In current terminology, "landed immigrant" and "illegal immigrant" are no longer used, and have been replaced with "permanent resident" and "undocumented immigrant," respectively. Immigration Canada is now known as Canada Citizenship and Immigration.

5. While it would be unfair to charge Foster with didacticism, it is also true that Foster states in his memoir, *Island Wings*, published after *Sleep on, Beloved*, that when he gave up teaching and entered journalism, he saw his new career as an opportunity to educate (223). I would argue that Foster's fiction also serves that purpose, in much the same way as Toni Morrison's *Beloved* or Barbara Kingsolver's *The Poisonwood Bible*.

6. This is not to be interpreted as my opposing a woman's right to abort when she deems it necessary. My point is that in Ona's belief system abortion is wrong; and because she had not yet worked through such beliefs, they still structured her psyche.

"The Multinational's Song": M G Vassanji's Work in Canadian Context

1. This essay is an updated and revised version of "'The Multinational's ong: The Global Reception of M.G. Vassanji" previously published in *The Global Reception of Post-liberalization Indian Novels in English* edited by Aysha Viswamohan, New Delhi: Anthem-Wimbledon, 2013. Updated July 2017.

2. From a 2010 iteration of the author website.

3. I use the large umbrella term (as employed by Vassanji) to include Michael Ondaatje, Rohinton Mistry, Himani Bannerji, Zulfikar Ghose, Uma Parmaswaran, Suwanda HJ Sugunasiri, Shauna Singh Baldwin, Anita Rau Badami, Arun Mukherjee, Ashok Mathur, Himani Bannerjee, David Chariandy, Neil Bissoondath, Cyril Dabydeen, Arnold Itwaru, Harold Sonny Ladoo, Sam Selvon, and Shani Mootoo, among many others.

4. TSAR Books. "Welcome to TSAR Publications." Online http://www.tsar-

books.com. Accessed 12 June 2010

5. Mawenzi House website http://www.mawenzihouse.com/Mawenzi_About.htm. Accessed 15 July 2017.

6. See, for instance, Martin Genetsch, *The Texture of Identity: The Fiction of MG Vassanji, Neil Bissoondath, and Rohinton Mistry*. TSAR Publications, 2007.

7. Website Penguin India. Online http://www.penguinbooksindia.com/category/Fiction/The_Gunny_Sack_9780143065692.aspx. Accessed 14 June 2010.

8. Importantly, as I am arguing the centrality of Vassanji's work for contemporary Canadian literature, others have argued about his significance in the framework of African literatures. Vassanji is often included in overviews of East African literature, as with Gikandi's *Columbia Guide*. In *Literature of Africa*, G D Killam argues that he "has established himself through his publication of six novels . . . as a major African writer" and proclaims that "Vassanji is the finest authentic voice of Asian Africans" (Killam, G D. *The Literature of Africa*. Greenwood Publishing Group 2004, p. 28).

9. Details at Statistics Canada. "Recent Immigrants to Canada, by region of origin: Chart 13.1."; see also, "Ethnic Diversity and Immigration" (2007). Online: http://www41.statcan.gc.ca/2007/30000/ceb30000_000-eng.htm (Accessed 14 May 2010) and http://www12.statcan.gc.ca/nhs-enm/2011/as-sa/99-010-x/99-010-x2011001-eng.cfm#a2. Accessed 15 July 2017.

10. In an interview with Allan Gregg, Vassanji notes that "the term Hindu is a modern term so for me having lived away and not also being part of the politics, the modern politics of hatred that has existed since 1947, I prefer the term Indian to Hindu or Muslim." (Gregg, Allan. "Interview with M G Vassanji." TV Ontario. www.youtube.com/watch?v=a0sCN8jz2Rk. Originally aired 29 March 2009. Accessed June 2010.)

11. In North America, the success of critics like Homi Bhabha, Gayatri Spivak, Harish Trivedi, Partha Chatterjee, Meenakshi Mukherjee, and C D Narasimhaiah before them, has been instrumental in mainstreaming postcolonial theory.

12. Vassanji, M.G. (2009) "Some personal Notes on the Books." Online: http://www.mgvassanji.com/PersonalNotes1.htm. Accessed 15 June 2010.

13. Gregg, Allan. "Interview with M G Vassanji." TV Ontario. www.youtube.com/watch?v=a0sCN8jz2Rk. Originally aired March 29, 2009. Accessed 15 June 2010.

References

"This dock is my dock": Dionne Brand's Room of Light

Agamben, Giorgio. *Infancy and History. On the Destruction of Experience*. Verso, 2007.

Anderson, Iain. *This is Our Music: Free Jazz, the Sixties, and American Culture*. University of Pennsylvania Press, 2007.

Arendt, Hannah. Introduction. Walter Benjamin. *Illuminations*. Edited and with an introduction by Hannah Arendt. Translated by Harry Zohn. Fontana, 1973.

Bhambra, Gurminder K. *Rethinking Modernity. Postcolonialism and the Sociological Imagination*. Palgrave Macmillan, 2007.

Belknap, Robert E. *The List. The Uses and Pleasures of Cataloguing*. Yale University Press, 2004.

Benjamin, Walter. "On Some Motifs in Baudelaire." Walter Benjanin. *Illuminations*. Edited and with an introduction by Hannah Arendt. Translated by Harry Zohn. Fontana, 1973.

Blanchard, Pascal, et al. "Human Zoos: the Greatest Exotic Shows in the West." *Human Zoos: Science and Spectacle in the Age of Colonial Empires*, edited by Pascal Blanchard, et al. Translated by Teresa Bridgeman. Liverpool University Press, 2008.

Brand, Dionne. *The Blue Clerk*. Unpublished work. To be published 2018 by McClelland & Stewart and Duke University Press.

———. *Inventory*. McClelland & Stewart, 2006.

———. *A Map to the Door of No Return: Notes to Belonging*. Doubleday Canada, 2001.

———. *Ossuaries*. McClelland & Stewart, 2010.

———. "To Promote Statements That Don't Have an End: In Conversation with Dionne Brand." Interview with E Martin Nolan. *Puritan* 11, Summer-Fall 2010, http://puritan-magazine.com/issue-xi-summerfall-2010/. Accessed 8

December 2012.
Coleman, Ornette. "Prime Time for Harmolodics." *Down Beat,* July 1983. 30 June 2016.
Deely, John. *Semiotic Animal: a Postmodern Definition of "Human Being" Transcending Patriarchy and Feminism.* St Augustine, 2005.
Fanon, Franz. *Black Skin, White Masks.* Grove Weidenfeld, 1967.
Kearney, Richard. "What is Diacritical Hermeneutics?" *Journal of Applied Hermeneutics,* December 10, 2011.
Lafuente, Antonio and Nuria Valverde. "Linnaean Botany and Spanish Imperial Biopolitics." *Colonial Botany: Science, Commerce, and Politics in the Early Modern World,* edited by Londa Schiebinger and Claudia Swan. University of Pennsylvania Press, 2005.
McCleary, Richard C. "Translator's Preface." *Signs,* by Maurice Merleau-Ponty. Translated, with an introduction, by Richard C McCleary. Northwestern University Press, 1964.
Merleau-Ponty, Maurice. *Signs.* Translated, with an introduction, by Richard C. McCleary. Northwestern University Press, 1964.
Müller-Willie, Staffan. "Walnuts at Hudson Bay, Coral reefs in Gotland. The colonialism of Linnaean Botany." *Colonial Botany: Science, Commerce, and Politics in the Early Modern World,* edited by Londa Schiebinger and Claudia Swan. University of Pennsylvania Press, 2005.
Richter, Gerhard. "Acts of self-portraiture: Benjamin's confessional and literary writings." *The Cambridge Companion to Walter Benjamin,* edited by David S Ferries. Cambridge University Press, 2004.
Sanders, Leslie. "Austin Clarke's Poetic Turn." *Confluences 1: Essays on the New Canadian Literature,* edited by Nurjehan Aziz. Mawenzi House Publishers, 2016.
Schiebinger, Londa and Claudia Swan. Introduction. *Colonial Botany: Science, Commerce, and Politics in the Early Modern World,* edited by Londa Schiebinger and Claudia Swan. University of Pennsylvania Press, 2005.
Sharpe, Christina. *In the Wake: On Blackness and Being.* Duke University Press, 2016.
Trouillot, Michel-Rolph. *Silencing the past: Power and the Production of History.* Beacon Press, 1995.
Violi, Patrizia. *Significato ed esperienza.* Bompiani, 1997.
von Uexküll, Jacob. *Ambienti animali e ambienti umani: Una passeggiata in mondi sconosciuti e invisibili.* Edited and translated by Marco Mazzeo. Quodlibet, 2010.
Watkins, Paul. "Listening to a Listening: the Disruptive Jazz Poetics of Dionne Brand's *Ossuaries* (A Call Towards Freedom)." *Critical Perspectives on Dionne Brand,* edited by Leslie Sanders and Heather Smyth. *MaComère* 14, (1&2), 2013-2014.

Between (Hi)Story and Space: Wayson Choy's Postmodern Chinatown

Anderson, Kay J. "The Idea of Chinatown: The Power of Place and Institutional Practice in the Making of a Racial Category." *Annals of the Association of American Geographers* 77.4, 1987.
Ang, Ien. *On Not Speaking Chinese: Living Between Asia and the West*. Routledge, 2005.
Choy, Wayson. *All That Matters: A Novel*. Anchor Canada, 2011.
———. *Not Yet: A Memoir of Living and Almost Dying*. Doubleday Canada, 2009.
———. *Paper Shadows: A Chinatown Childhood*. Viking, 1999.
———. *The Jade Peony: A Novel*. Douglas & McIntyre, 1995.
De Certeau, Michel. *The Practice of Everyday Life*. Translated by Steven F Rendall. University of California Press, 2011.
Deer, Glenn, and Wayson Choy. "An Interview with Wayson Choy." *Canadian Literature* 163, 1999.
Khoo, Tseen-Ling. *Banana Bending: Asian-Australian and Asian-Canadian Literatures*. McGill-Queen's Press, 2003.
Lee, Christopher. "Engaging Chineseness in Wayson Choy's The Jade Peony." *Canadian Literature* 163, 1999.
Lefebvre, Henri. *The Production of Space*. Wiley-Blackwell, 1992.
Lowe, Lisa. *Immigrant Acts: On Asian American Cultural Politics*. Duke University Press, 1996.
Reed, Brad, and Wayson Choy. "Wayson Choy: Mastering the Moment." *Humber Literary Review* 1.1, Spring/Summer 2014.

Landscape and Diasporic Citizenship(s) in Ramabai Espinet's *The Swinging Bridge* and *Nuclear Seasons*

Ashcroft, Bill. *Post-Colonial Transformation*. Routledge, 2001.
Ashcroft, Bill, Gareth Griffiths and Helen Tiffin, editors. *The Postcolonial studies Reader*. Routledge, 1995.
Brah, Artar. *Cartographies of Diaspora Contesting Identities (Gender, Racism, Ethnicity)*, Routledge, 1996.
Birbalsingh, Singh. "South Asian Canadian Writers from Africa and the Caribbean." *Canadian Literature: A Quarterly of Criticism and Review* 132, 1992.
———. "South Asian Canadian Novels in English". *A Meeting of Streams: South Asian Canadian Literature*. Mawenzi House Publishers, 1985.
———. "Indo-Trinidadian Identities and Sexuality: A Survey of Shani Mootoo's Fiction." *Critical Perspectives on Indo-Caribbean Women's Literature*, edited by Joy Mahabir and Mariam Pirbhai, Routledge, 2013.
Carter, Paul. *Living in a New Country. History, Travelling and Language*. Faber & Faber, 1992.
Chambers, Iain. *Migrancy, Culture, Identity*. Routledge, 1994.
Conway, Dennis. "Migration Trends in the Americas." *Revisiting the Americas: Teaching and Learning the Geography of the Western Hemispheres*, edited by

Tom Martinson. National Council for Geographic Education, 1992.
Dascălu, Cristina Emanuela. *Imaginary Homelands of Writers in Exile Salman Rushdie, Bharati Mukherjee, and V. S Naipaul.* Cambria Press, 2007.
Espinet, Ramabai. *Nuclear Seasons Poetry by Ramabai Espinet.* Sister Vision, 1991.
———. *The Swinging Bridge.* HarperCollins, 2003.
Fanon, Frantz. *The Wretched of the Earth.* Grove Press, 2009.
Glissant, Édouard. *Poetics of Relation.* Translated by Betsy Wing. University of Michigan Press, 1997.
Hall, Stuart. "Minimal Selves." *Identity: The Real Me. Post-Modernism and the Question of Identity,* ICA Documents 6, ICA, 1987.
Heidegger, Martin. "Letter on Humanism." *Basic Writings,* Harper Perennial Modern Classics, 2008.
Ogborn, M. "The Relations between Geography and History: Work in Historical Geography in 1997." *Progress in Human Geography* 23.
Ramraj, Victor. "Still Arriving: the Assimilationist Indo-Caribbean Experience of Marginality." *Reworlding the Literature of the Indian Diaspora,* edited by Emmanuel S. Nelson, Greenwood Press, 1992.
Said, Edward. "Reflections on Exile." *Out There, Marginalization and Contemporary Cultures,* edited by Russell Ferguson, Martha Gever, Trinh T Minh-ha and Cornell West, MIT Press, 1990.
———. *Culture and Imperialism,* Vintage, 1999.
Solbaic, Rodolphe. "Revising Female Indian Memory Ramabai Espinet's Reconstruction of an Indo-Trinidadian Diaspora in *The Swinging Bridge.*" *Critical Perspectives on Indo-Caribbean Literature,* edited by Joy Mahabir and Mariam Pirbhai, Routledge, 2013.
———. *Émergence d'une identité caribéenne canadienne anglophone.* L'Harmattan, 2015.
Tolia-Kelly, Divya P. *Landscape, Race and Memory: Material Ecologies of Citizenship,* Ashgate, 2010.

Cecil Foster's *Sleep on, Beloved*: Reflections on Afro-Caribbean Immigrant Existence in Toronto

Aird, Paula. *What Goes Around . . .* Trafford, 2004.
Brand, Dionne. *What We All Long For.* Knopf, 2005.
———. *A Map to the Door of No Return: Notes on Belonging.* Doubleday, 2001.
———. *In Another Place, not Here.* Vintage, 1997.
Clarke, Austin. *The Meeting Point* [1967]. Vintage, 1998.
———. *Storm of Fortune* [1973]. Vintage, 1998.
———. *The Bigger Light* [1975]. Vintage, 1998.
Dorsinville, Max. *Erzulie Loves Shango.* CIDIHCA, 1998.
DuBois, W E B. *The Souls of Black Folk* [1903]. *Three Negro Classics,* edited by John Hope Franklin. Avon Books, 1965.
Foster, Cecil. Interview. *Why We Write: Conversations with African Canadian Poets and Novelists,* edited by H Nigel Thomas. TSAR Publications, 2006.

———. *Where Race Does not Matter: The New Spirit of Modernity.* Penguin, 2005.
———. *Island Wings.* HarperCollins, 1998.
———. *A Place Called Heaven: The Meaning of Being Black in Canada.* HarperCollins, 1996.
———. *Sleep on, Beloved.* Random House, 1995.
———. *No Man in the House.* Random House, 1991.
Itwaru, Arnold Harrichand. *Home and Back.* TSAR Publications, 2001.
———. *The Invention of Canada: Literary Text and the Immigrant Imaginary.* TSAR Publications, 1990.
Philip, M. Nourbese. *Harriet's Daughter.* Women's Press, 1988.
———. *Frontiers: Essays and Writings on Racism and Culture.* Mecury, 1992.
Prince, Althea. *Loving This Man.* Insomniac Press, 2001.
Silvera, Makeda. *The Heart Does not Bend.* Random House, 2002.
———. *Silenced: Talks with Working Class West Indian Women about Their Lives as Domestic Workers in Canadá.* Williams-Wallace, 1983.
Sinclair, Upton. *The Jungle* [1906]. Penguin, 1987.
Vassanji, M G. *No New Land.* McClelland & Stewart, 1991.
Warriar. Nalini. *The Enemy Within.* TSAR Publications, 2005.

"The Multinational's Song": M G Vassanji's Work in Canadian Context

Gikandi, Simon and Evan Mwangi. *The Columbia Guide to East African Literature in English Since 1945.* Columbia University Press, 2007.
Killam, G D. *The Literature of Africa.* Greenwood Publishing Group, 2004.
Mukherjee, Arun. *Postcolonialism: My Living.* TSAR Publications, 1998.
Vassanji, M G. *A Meeting of Streams: South Asian-Canadian Literature.* Toronto: TSAR 1998
———. "*Am I a Canadian Writer?*" *Canadian Literature* 190, Autumn 2006.
Gregg, Allan. "Interview with M G Vassanji." TV Ontario. www.youtube.com/watch?v=a0sCN8jz2Rk. Originally aired March 29, 2009. Accessed 15 June 2010.

Dismantled Domestics, Loneliness, and Creative Coping in Rabindranath Maharaj's *The Amazing Absorbing Boy*

Heinrich, Liesl M and Eleonora Gullone. "The clinical significance of loneliness: A literature review." *Clinical Psychology Review* 26, 2006.
Long, Christopher R et al. "Solitude Experiences: Varieties, Settings, and Individual Differences." *Personality and Social Psychology Bulletin* 29:5, 2003.
Maharaj, Rabindranath. *The Amazing Absorbing Boy.* Vintage Canada, 2010.
Winnicott, D W, "The Capacity To Be Alone." *The International Journal of Psycho-Analysis* 39, 1958.
Winton, Alexa Griffith. "Inhabited Space: Critical Theories and the Domestic Interior." *The Handbook of Interior Architecture and Design*, Bloomsbury Press, 2013.

A Long Journey to Mercy: Joy Kogawa's *Gently to Nagasaki*

Caruth, Cathy, editor. *Listening to Trauma: Conversations with Leaders in the Theory and Treatment of Catastrophic Experience*. Johns Hopkins UP, 2014.

Cook, Rufus. "'The Penelope Work of Forgetting': Dreams, Memory, and the Recovery of Wholeness in Joy Kogawa's *Obasan*." *College Literature* 34.3, 2007.

Hernandez, Jon. "Gently to Nagasaki: Celebrated Canadian Author Joy Kogawa Releases Memoir." Sept. 22, 2016. http://www.cbc.ca/news/canada/british-columbia/gently-to-nagasaki-celebrated-canadian-author-joy-kogawa-releases-memoir-1.3774333

Kogawa, Joy. *Gently to Nagasaki*. Caitlin Press, 2016.

———. *The Rain Ascends*. 1995. Revised edition. Penguin, 2003.

———. *Itsuka*. Anchor, 1994.

———. *Obasan*. Penguin, 1983.

———. "Is There a Just Cause?" *Up and Doing: Canadian Women and Peace*, edited by Janice Williamson and Deborah Gorham. Women's Press, 1989.

Lefebvre , Benjamin. "In Search of Someday: Trauma and Repetition in Joy Kogawa's Fiction." *Journal of Canadian Studies* 44.3, 2010.

Shoenut, Meredith L. "'I Am Canadian': Truth of Citizenship in Joy Kogawa's *Obasan*." *American Review of Canadian Studies* 36.3, 2006.

Sywenky, Irene. "Recovering the Voice of the Japanese-Canadian Community: History and Private and Public Discourses in J Kogawa's Poetry and Prose." Special issue *Asian Pacific Diaspora and Contemporary Asian-Canadian Literature*, edited by Peng-xiang Chen and I-Chun Wang. *Canadian Review of Comparative Literature/Revue Canadienne de Littérature Comparée* 36.3, 2009.

Turcotte, Gerry. "'Horror Written on Their Skin': Joy Kogawa's Gothic Uncanny." *Unsettled Remains: Canadian Literature and the Postcolonial Gothic*, edited by Cynthia Conchita Sugars and Gerry Turcotte. WLU Press, 2009.

Gendered Violence and Feminist Interventions in Shauna Singh Baldwin's *The Selector of Souls*

Baldwin, Shauna Singh. *The Selector of Souls*. Vintage, 2012.

Beauvoir, Simone. *The Second Sex*. Vintage, 1968.

D'Cruze, S and A Rao. "Violence and the Vulnerabilities of Gender." *Violence, Vulnerability and Embodiment: Gender and History*, edited by S D'Cruze and A Rao. Blackwell Publishing, 2005.

Ghosh, Bishnupriya, and Brinda Bose, editors. *Interventions: Feminist Dialogues on Third World Women's Literature and Film*. Garland Publishing Inc, 1997.

Jia Lisa Lau Ee. "Equating Womanhood with Victimhood: The Positionality of Women Protagonists in the Contemporary Writings of South Asian Women." *Women's Studies International Forum* 26.4, 2003.

Menon, Ritu, and Kamla Bhasin. *Borders and Boundaries: Women in India's Partition*. Rutgers UP, 1998.

Mohanty, Chandra Talpade. *Feminism Without Borders: Decolonizing Theory,*

Practicing Solidarity. Duke UP, 2003.

———, et al, editors. *Third World Women and the Politics of Feminism*. Indiana UP, 1991.

Sangha, Jagjit K, and Tahira Gonsalves. Introduction. *South Asian Mothering: Negotiating Culture, Family and Selfhood*. Demeter Press, 2013.

Sayed, Asma. "Postcolonial Mothering in Anita Rau Badami's *Tamarind Mem*." *Confluences 1: Essays on New Canadian Literature*, edited by Nurjehan Aziz. Mawenzi House, 2016.

Tharu, Susie, and K Lalita, editors. *Women Writing in India: 600BC to the Present*. Feminist Press, 1991-93.

Watts, C, and C Zimmerman. "Violence Against Women: Global Scope and Magnitude." *The Lancet* 359, 2002.

Contributors

FRANCA BERNABEI taught English and postcolonial literatures at Ca'Foscari University (Venice, Italy) and was more recently an exchange professor at Louisiana State University (Baton Rouge). She has published essays and articles on migrant, transatlantic, and diasporic Caribbean literatures both in Italy and abroad. She is the author of two books, one of which is focused on Jean Rhys.

SHOILEE KHAN is a doctoral student in English Literature at York University. Her fiction appears in the short story collection *The Unpublished City* (BookThug, 2017) and in diverse magazines and journals. She was long-listed for the 2017 CBC short fiction prize and is serving as a member of the Planning Committee for the Festival of Literary Diversity. She also teaches English in the School of Communication and Literary Studies at Sheridan College.

DANNABANG KUWABONG teaches Caribbean literature at the University of Puerto Rico, San Juan. He has published three books: *Konga and other Dagaaba Folktales*, *Visions of Venom*, *Caribbean Blues & Love's Genealogy*, *Echoes from Dusty Rivers*, and *Voices from Kibuli Country*.

LAURA MOSS is associate professor at the University of British Columbia, specializing in postcolonial African and Canadian Literatures. She has co-edited five books, published numerous articles, and is the Editor of the journal *Canadian Literature*.

ASMA SAYED is a professor of English at Kwantlen Polytechnic University. Her research focuses on Indian Ocean Studies, Postcolonial Literature, and the South Asian diaspora in Canada. Her latest books include: *Screening Motherhood in*

Contemporary World Cinema (2016); *M G Vassanji: Essays on His Works* (2014); and *Writing Diaspora: Transnational Memories, Identities, and Cultures* (2014).

Irene Sywenky is associate professor of Comparative Literature at the University of Alberta. She has published on postcolonial and post-imperial cultural spaces in Central Europe; border identities and border cultures; memory; cultural translation; popular culture; and contemporary Canadian literature. She has co-edited various collections and special journal issues, and her articles have appeared in edited volumes and international journals. She is currently the editor of the *Canadian Review of Comparative Literature.*

H Nigel Thomas was a teacher with the Protestant School Board of Greater Montreal, before joining the faculty at Laval University, Quebec, from where he recently retired. His published works of fiction include *Behind the Face of Winter; Return to Arcadia Lives; Whole and Otherwise;* and *When the Bottom Falls Out.*

Jason Wang is a doctoral candidate (ABD) in Communication and Culture at York University and an Executive Member of the Modern Literature and Culture Research Centre at Ryerson University. His dissertation, "Urban Walking: Configuring the Modern City as Cultural and Spatial Practice," addresses the politics of spatial aesthetics in modernist and contemporary urban literature and culture. His review essays have been published in *Canadian Literature* and *Studies in American Naturalism.*